PATRIOT REIGN

PATRIOT REIGN

*Bill Belichick, the Coaches,
and the Players
Who Built a Champion*

Michael Holley

wm
William Morrow
An Imprint of **HarperCollins***Publishers*

JH

HarperCollins books may be purchased for educational, business, or sales promotional use. For information please write: Special Markets Department, HarperCollins Publishers Inc., 10 East 53rd Street, New York, NY 10022.

FIRST EDITION

Designed by Paula Szafranski

Printed on acid-free paper

Library of Congress Cataloging-in-Publication Data has been applied for.

ISBN 0-06-075794-9

04 05 06 07 08 WBC/RRD 10 9 8 7 6 5 4 3

For Marilyn Holley, who always
finds gems in the clutter

CONTENTS

INTRODUCTION

Two years ago I sat in Bill Belichick's office and talked with him about an idea I had for a book. I told the head coach of the New England Patriots that I was interested in examining several aspects of NFL culture through the eyes of his organization. It would be a book that would give readers an access pass to places from which they are usually forbidden. They would be able to see candid glimpses of a team, from ownership to coaching to playing. They would sit in meeting rooms, watch games from the coaches' box, learn about scouting, and ultimately better understand the cerebral man who is often called the best coach in the National Football League.

Belichick listened to the proposal and rubbed his forehead. Not wanting to hear his answer then, I kept talking.

I was a general sports columnist for the *Boston Globe* at the time, so I wanted to assure him that such a project would require a one-year leave from the paper. It would be impossible for me to immerse myself in the NFL for most of the day and continue to write a column in the remaining hours. The coach needed to be convinced, for example, that his private conversations with head trainer Jim Whalen would not wind up as part of my sports discussions in print or on the air. I told him that I wouldn't do any media work while the Patriots were in season.

After I finished my pitch, Belichick sat in the chair, with his right foot touching the floor and his left heel on the edge of the seat. He was quiet for what seemed like five minutes.

"I'll have to talk with Robert about it," he said finally, referring to team owner Robert Kraft. "But it sounds good to me."

It wasn't exactly what I had expected to hear; I was sure he was going to say "No, thanks."

Belichick talked with Kraft, and I was given permission to shadow the team. What followed was one of the most educational, entertaining, and humbling years of my life. I was able to sit in corners and observe the think tank that is football operations in Foxboro, Massachusetts. I quickly noticed that under Belichick the Patriots have one of the most unusual workplaces in America. It is difficult to find the office slacker who turns instant messaging into a full-time job. Belichick has surrounded himself with smart, competent people who are encouraged to be original thinkers—so original that if their analyses are different from those of the boss, they are encouraged to disagree with him. Belichick has no problem listening to any counterargument—provided that it can be supported with some type of evidence.

INTRODUCTION

As I sat in those corners, trying to blend in and take notes at the same time, I kept waiting for someone to ask me to leave *that* out of the book. There was usually an explicit description in a meeting, and a few times there were energetic exchanges between coaches. But the tap on the shoulder never came from anyone in the organization. I was sure it was going to come in January 2003, when an agitated Belichick began talking about his defensive backs in a player evaluation meeting. He had expected more out of a unit that included Lawyer Milloy, Tebucky Jones, and Victor Green. He saw their performance one way—not good—and defensive backs coach Eric Mangini was on the other side of the argument. With voices raised, they both defended their positions. Mangini insisted that Green was one of the best playmakers on the team, and Belichick said he was too slow. They went back and forth until Belichick asked Josh McDaniels, who was a coaching assistant at the time, to go to the computer system. He wanted McDaniels to retrieve some plays "from the Buffalo game."

"Which Buffalo game, Coach?" McDaniels asked.

"Either one," Belichick said. "There's enough bad shit to look at in either game."

The exchange between Belichick and Mangini lasted for about ten minutes. And then it was over. There is very little carryover in Foxboro. You say what needs to be said, and then you move on. I had become accustomed to the intense football operations culture, and it had become accustomed to me. That was obvious when Belichick introduced a new quarterbacks coach, John Hufnagel, to the staff in 2003.

"John, you've met everyone here, right?" Belichick said.

"Yes," Hufnagel replied. "Everyone but the gentleman in the corner."

INTRODUCTION

He was talking about me. After my presence caused some early awkward moments, I had become part of the wallpaper. "Oh, him?" a couple of the coaches laughed. "That's just Michael."

After the Patriots finished the 2002 season with a 9–7 record, a few players and coaches were almost apologetic about what would become of the book. They knew that the story of a nonplay-off team, one season removed from winning Super Bowl XXXVI, wouldn't excite many publishers. I told them that I was going to continue to work on it, and that everything could be salvaged if the Patriots could find a way to win Super Bowl XXXVIII. Even though it wasn't part of the initial plan, Belichick never cut off my access as the 2002 season became the 2003 season. Every once in a while he would ask, "How's the book?" and I would answer with a sigh.

That changed in October 2003, when the Patriots won their first of fifteen consecutive games. Indeed, they capped the season with a win over the Carolina Panthers in Super Bowl XXXVIII. "Well," Belichick said then. "I don't have to ask you about the book now. It looks like you have it."

Boston, 2004

PATRIOT REIGN

THE ART OF THE GAME

Bill Belichick has moments that few people see or imagine, moments when he is no longer the premier strategist of his profession. These are the times when he could be the guy in the next cubicle, any other father, husband, or son. These breaks from brilliance make him a stronger coach. They remind him that briefly stepping away from his football vision can actually allow him to see more of it.

There are times when the diagrammed plays on the erasable board in his office are for an audience of two—his sons, Stephen and Brian. There are times when the brainteasers he attempts to solve are provided by members of his family, not by other coaches. "Do you know what 'discrete' means?" he said one day after a conversation with

Brian. His younger son—who attends Brookline's Dexter School, John F. Kennedy's alma mater—was studying vocabulary words. "Discrete" was one of them. "It's not the same as 'discreet,'" Belichick said. "Brian's class is going over words that have similar sounds with different meanings. That's a good one."

There was the time he tried to put on one of his favorite sweaters and could barely get it over his shoulders. Laundry mistake. He called his wife, Debby, to talk about it. He heard a lot of laughter coming from the phone. "It's not funny," he said with a smirk, even though he knew it was.

What most surprises people who don't know him is how much he enjoys a good laugh, usually when he's away from work and sometimes when he's at it. He earned a reputation for giving bland descriptions during his press conferences, where his personality is the sacrifice to protecting the goods. Press conferences are part of his game plans—he prepares for them at least fifteen to twenty minutes per day—so he is especially conscious of saying or implying anything that will give an opponent an edge. By the time he walks into his morning briefings with the New England media, he has already broken them down. He has predicted the incendiary topics of the day, sketched an outline of how he will respond to those topics, and offered suggestions to his players on how they should respond too. He has mastered an indifferent *look* during these conferences, yet when they are over he can easily recall details about late-arriving reporters, opinion-makers he hasn't seen in a while, and questioners he didn't recognize. When his conversation is no longer on the record, it's as if some hidden masseuse has suddenly relieved him of tension points.

He can be relaxed during television production meetings, depending on the broadcast crew for the game. He's been extremely loose with Phil Simms, Greg Gumbel, and Armen Keteyian of CBS. He trusts them enough to joke with them. Once he went into a meeting seeing if he could needle Simms. "Phil, I've heard you've been ripping the shit out of me," he said to the former Giants quarterback. "That's all I hear from people: 'Simms is ripping your ass during the broadcast.'" Simms didn't fall for it. He knew that Belichick wouldn't leave anything to hearsay and that if he had indeed ripped Belichick, the coach would know exactly when it happened, down and distance included. "Bullshit," Simms said. "All I do is talk about how smart you are. We call you the smartest coach ever every week." Belichick laughed, leaned back in his chair, and acted as if he were getting ready for a card game with his friends.

It helps that Simms has known Belichick since 1979, but that's not the only reason Belichick respects him and his crew. He is even more impressed with their preparation. They are often dressed casually in these meetings—T-shirts, baseball caps, flip-flops—but they always have a plan for what is going to be discussed. Simms is indeed their quarterback, so they all watch film and jot down observations to present to Belichick. Their hard work makes him so comfortable that he often sits in the meetings, feet propped up, telling stories. He once told them that he ran a marathon and was spotted by Giants fans. "They saw me, and one fan says, 'Look, there's Belichick of the Giants. They still don't have a running game!'"

On some days when things are quiet at Gillette Stadium—after the Saturday morning walk-through and before the Saturday evening coaches' meeting—Belichick is visited by one of his three dogs. Sometimes he entertains

Tom Brady—a sports fan with an appreciation of sports history—by telling tales about the old Giants. He once called defensive lineman Richard Seymour into his office so they could watch tape and talk about some of the dominant players of the NFC East in the 1980s.

He may have been born in Tennessee and raised in Maryland, but he's got a lot of Northeast humor in him. He can be clever, sarcastic, and profane. Coming from his office it's not unusual to hear the voices of Frank Rizzo and Sol Rosenberg, the characters dreamed up by the Jerky Boys, the notorious telephone pranksters from Queens. When he isn't listening to their funny stories, he tells a few of his own. He tells one about a family vacation in Europe in the mid-1990s. No matter where they went, the Belichicks saw dozens of Europe's aged churches. They saw landmarks and a certain recurring icon. At one point Brian turned to his parents and said, "Who is this guy? We're seeing him everywhere."

The "guy" was Jesus Christ.

"I don't know if I should tell that story," Belichick says, shaking his head. "People are going to think we're bad parents."

He has gone from twenty-six-year-old coach-peer to fifty-two-year-old coach-teacher. He has learned to be more of a negotiator with his own team, making compromises in some areas—or at least being able to listen—without selling out his core beliefs. He no longer has to worry about the potential conflicts of interest that he encountered in Baltimore, Detroit, Denver, and the early days of New York. He was a young coach then, either the same age or just a couple of years older than the players who reported to him. He has an understanding and respect for issues now that he didn't after the 1989 season, when he had his first head-coaching interview. The Phoenix Cardinals were interested in talking to him then. The team had moved from St. Louis one year earlier, and ownership wanted someone who would go from city to city in Arizona, helping to promote the team.

"I didn't realize how much they were looking for that," Belichick says. "You know, I figured winning would generate the interest as opposed to going out and doing little rallies." It's not what the Cardinals wanted to hear. They gave the job to Joe Bugel. It would be years before Belichick would develop a head coach's scope of vision, years before he would see that planning the issues around the game is as important as planning the game itself.

"Let's put it this way: when you're the head coach, you're the head coach twenty-four hours a day, seven days a week. No matter what happens, it's on your watch and, to a degree, it's your problem," he says. "It doesn't matter what. Some guy can run a stop sign and get pulled over by the police, and they're calling you. If the fertilizer doesn't come and the grass is going to be brown, you might get a call, 'What are we going to do?' It's everything."

Early in his head-coaching career he couldn't resist obsessing over minutiae. He would sit in on the Cleveland Browns' defensive meetings and talk about how a pattern should be covered. He would pop into special-teams meetings and talk about punt-protection techniques. He would map out the offensive game plan because, for two seasons, he was also his team's offensive coordinator. He was a coaching phenom, a young fastballer who didn't know how to change speeds. The joy to him then, at thirty-nine, was the pure rush of coaching. It was the ideal of coaching in a vacuum, having a vision with no periphery required. But it really was an ideal. Thinking like a football CEO is part of the job. Allowing the media glimpses of the team and being cooperative in the daily dance with them is part of the job. He underestimated the importance of that in Cleveland, and he was generally resented for it.

"When I got there, there had been a very open media policy from previous regimes. They had open practices, open locker rooms, pretty much whatever they wanted, to the point where the players really had no privacy. You know, a guy would play a joke on somebody or say something and it would be in the paper the next day. There was no real opportunity for the team to build much of its own personality or chemistry because that stuff was reported on a daily basis.

"I clamped down on them. It could have been done in a more positive or gracious way. I could have made some concessions so that it wouldn't have come off as being so harsh. I take responsibility for it. But the bottom line was we just didn't win quickly enough. The media logic was 'Okay, you want to come in and close practices and limit our access and give us some short answers? You had better start putting up some wins.' And when that didn't happen, with three consecutive losing seasons, there wasn't a great defense mechanism built up there.

"But I was kind of oblivious to that too. Because I really was more concerned about coaching the team than trying to be a PR machine."

Back then he didn't have someone taping the Sunday night wrap-up shows on local TV, as he does now. Unlike today, he didn't have a thick pack of local and national newspaper clips that he would read as he worked out on a treadmill. He didn't have someone to not only monitor the discussions on sports-talk radio but also filter the volume and give him any items of significance. He didn't have radio personalities and columnists freely saying "In Bill We Trust," as is the case in New England. He had more to prove then, in an organization that would prove to be less competent and unified than the one he's in now.

For Belichick, there was always the game. But with each addition to his personal and professional timeline, he began to see it from new angles. A lot happened in the twenty years between his ambitious start in Baltimore in 1975 and his employer's shocking announcement that it was moving to Baltimore—he guessed that the moving trucks would take off without him—in 1995. One day in his early twenties he is living at Howard Johnson's and driving Baltimore Colts head coach Ted Marchibroda to work. Then one day in his late thirties he is flying into Cleveland and being shuttled to the Ritz Carlton, where Browns hats and sweatshirts are lying on his bed. He and Debby join Art Modell and his wife, Pat, at the Modells' home for dinner. Bill and Art go into the den, shape a contract, and agree to terms that will make him the coach of the Browns. Then one day in his early forties, one of the strangest days he's ever had, he learns midseason that his team is moving and finds himself calling a member of the media for insight.

He looked in the *Boston Globe* on November 4, 1995, and saw an article headlined "Browns Look to Baltimore." Will McDonough broke the story and began it by writing, "The Baltimore Browns. Get used to it." McDonough wrote that an announcement would be made in two days, on Monday, the day before the NFL owners were scheduled to meet in Dallas. "I saw the article and I'm thinking, *Wow.* I talked to Will, and Will said, 'Yeah, there's no doubt about it. This is what's going to happen.' Will had some good inside information. So that really kind of sent the antennas up." The lame-duck Browns had a home game the next day against Houston and were crushed, 37–10. They lost seven of their final eight games. "Modell" became a six-letter obscenity in Cleveland.

Four months after the announcement, Belichick was dismayed, though not surprised, when news of his job status was finally delivered. He knew he was going to be fired. It was the delivery of his firing that was problematic. "I'm sure there were things that I did that Art wasn't thrilled with, but I worked hard for him. I spent a lot of hours there, and I tried to do what was best for the team. And in typical Art fashion, five years later, it was just a phone call." During that call Belichick debated Modell on the wording of the proposed firing statement to the media. Belichick didn't like the way the document was phrased. He thought the statement was one-sided, a piece of propaganda that attempted to place all the organization's problems at his feet. He looked over the announcement and warned Modell, "If you release this statement, I'm going to release one and you're not going to like it. So let's try to come up with something that we can both live with."

The statement was changed. Both the Browns and Belichick would be moving. Marchibroda was going to return to Baltimore as coach of the new Ravens. And Belichick was going to pack his van and drive to New England. Miami Dolphins head coach Jimmy Johnson had talked with him about becoming defensive coordinator of the Dolphins, but Belichick had loved New England since prep school and college. He had homes on Nantucket, he had friends from high school and college in the area, and Bill Parcells had promised him a job as one of his Patriots assistants. Over the course of the next four years he would follow Parcells to the New York Jets as his defensive coordinator and assistant head coach, then return to New England, this time as head coach.

Maybe some people in Andover, Massachusetts, would have found this ironic in 1971. Maybe they would have been surprised to know that the long-haired center on the undefeated football team would one day be forty miles south, in Foxboro, the man with final say in football operations. But it wouldn't have seemed unusual to a nineteen-year-old Bill Belichick. Even at Andover he was a little different from the other students.

He listened to the Dead, James Taylor, Bob Dylan, and Simon & Garfunkel, as many of them did. He took similar classes and got similar grades—As and Bs—although it didn't come naturally to him. "When I walked into Andover, I was surrounded by a lot of people who were a whole lot smarter than I was," he says. "And they knew a lot more than I did on top of that. They had more experience than I did in terms of traveling and being exposed to a lot of different things. Academically, it was the hardest year I had in school. Way harder than college."

His prep school notebooks contained *Macbeth* study notes on one page and an imagined play—the football kind—on the next. He had taken four years of French in high school (Belichick attended Bates High School for one year and graduated from Annapolis High), but he still struggled with the language at Andover. He was assigned to read *Les Misérables* in French. He found himself looking up forty words per page. "It was unbelievable," he says. "Jean Valjean—I hated that fucker."

He grew up some at Andover. He met students who amazed him with their smarts. Whether they were writing, playing the saxophone, or acting, they were astonishing at what they did. For the first time Belichick asked for help in school. He went to teachers and other students when he came across something that was unfamiliar to him. Andover expanded his mind—and probably would have blown his parents' minds if they had known what he was experiencing.

"In all honesty, they probably didn't know exactly how liberal things were at Andover, and subsequently Wesleyan. You know, you send your kid off to prep schools back then, and you think there's some structure, and there was. But there was a lot of drug use in the dorms. It wasn't any big secret. I mean, some dorms were stricter than others, but I think there was quite a bit of drug use on campus from what I saw."

There were academic changes and social changes, but there were no athletic changes. He played football at Andover and knew he wanted to continue at Wesleyan. He didn't want to stop there. He and his friend Ernie Adams had already thought about careers in either college or pro coaching. They both graduated from college in 1975—Adams went to Northwestern—and decided to pursue long-term passion over short-term prestige. Adams, who grew up in Brookline, Massachusetts, took a job with the Patriots, the pro team down the road. Belichick wanted to get a master's degree in economics and be a graduate assistant on some college's staff.

He took what turned out to be a perfect job with the Baltimore Colts: $25 a week and the chance to absorb football every day from seven A.M. until midnight. He lived for free at the Howard Johnson's next to Baltimore-Washington International Airport. His boss, Marchibroda, knew the owner of the hotel and traded Colts tickets for four rooms. Marchibroda was in his first season with the Colts after being on George Allen's staff in Washington. He wasn't going to move his family from Washington to Baltimore, so he came up with the Howard Johnson's deal. Belichick, Marchibroda, and two other assistant coaches, George Boutselis and Whitey Dovell, all lived there. They would meet in the lobby at seven, go to breakfast—where Marchibroda would order the same thing every day—and talk about football.

Belichick was their driver on the way to the office. He was also in charge of film breakdowns, meticulously charting each play by down, formation, motion, and field position. His father, Steve, an assistant football coach for the U.S. Naval Academy Midshipmen, always believed that to be the best way to learn football. Belichick helped run the scout team and assisted with special teams. The only thing he didn't do was game plans. He was so good at what he did that his salary was doubled after training camp.

So now he was up to $2,400 a year—before taxes. He didn't mind the scant salary. Anyway, watching his father had taught him how to handle money. Steve Belichick didn't believe in credit and never bought anything on it. His philosophy was that you had the money or you didn't. And when the elder Belichick had it, he bought a piece of Annapolis land for $5,000 and built a $29,500 house on top of it. The Belichicks—Steve, Jeanette, and Bill—moved into the house when Bill was six years old. Bill's money was fine during the Colts' 10–4 regular season. But something had to change after the play-offs, when Baltimore was eliminated by the dominant Steelers, 28–10.

There would be no Howard Johnson's in the off-season. Which also meant that Marchibroda's car wouldn't be there to drive. Belichick was going to need a local apartment, a car, or both to keep the job. Marchibroda wanted him to stay, but general manager Joe Thomas said the team couldn't come up with an apartment, a car, or more money. These were the new Colts, owned by a man Baltimoreans would come to despise. His name was Robert Irsay. The Colts had traded Johnny Unitas and Mike Curtis, they had begun lobbying for a new stadium, and they couldn't find a way to keep a promising twenty-three-year-old coach on staff. Thomas even told Belichick to wait tables in the off-season because there wasn't much else a coach could do all winter until the first days of spring.

Thomas was wrong, of course, and a head coach named Rick Forzano knew it. Belichick called the Detroit Lions looking for a job, and Forzano offered this deal: $10,000 a year with a 1976 Thunderbird included. The kid needed a car? Well, the kid needed to work for the team that was owned by the Fords. Belichick did some work as an advance scout, coached tight ends, coached receivers, and spent a lot of time listening to the Lions' defensive coaches. Jerry Glanville was working with the linebackers; Fritz Shurmur's group was the defensive line; Jim Carr, "one of the top defensive coordinators at that time," was in the secondary; and Floyd Reese was assigned to the special-teamers. The offense had Joe Bugel and Ken Shipp, who had coached Joe Namath and John Riggins with the New York Jets.

"An all-star staff," Belichick says.

Some Detroit coaches would talk with Steve Belichick and report, "Your kid is something special. He's really unbelievable." The father would say then the same thing he says now: "Thanks. But he's never been accused of being a dummy." Forzano didn't get to witness the professional growth of Belichick for long, though. The team started 1–3 in '76, with all the losses to NFC Central teams, and Tommy Hudspeth became the coach. The Lions finished with back-to-back 6–8 seasons when Belichick was there. He was forced to leave his job and his Thunderbird after the '77 season.

He was four months away from his twenty-sixth birthday. He was unemployed. And he had been recently married to his friend from Annapolis High, an attractive young woman named Debby Clarke. Bill and Debby were married under the golden dome of the Naval Academy's chapel. They had their reception on campus as well, in the same hall where their prom had been held. They spent 1978 in Denver before moving back to the East Coast in 1979.

"By the time I got through with those four years, I felt I had been around the block on a lot of different levels," Belichick says. "I had seen a lot of different players and head-coaching styles. I had been in the AFC and NFC. I felt I had four good years studying special teams, two years studying offense, and two studying defense."

He had worked for four coaches in three cities. He was beginning to acquire the education that he couldn't get in school, no matter how prestigious those schools are. He was twenty-six years old, almost twenty-seven, and now he knew what it meant to take control of a meeting. He understood how dangerous it is to be surrounded by yes men, sycophants who silently nod along with you even though your premise or approach may be faulty. He saw how rapidly an employment status can change. Sometimes it's because the owners are cheap, sometimes it's because the owners want the teams to win more, and sometimes it just doesn't work.

Belichick was headed to New York, a city where he would become idolized as a prepared and visionary coach. In exactly twenty years he would go to court for the right to leave New York. It wouldn't be leaving New York as much as it would be professionally separating himself from Bill Parcells, a boss with whom he was tired of being associated. One day he would feel as if he were an established country that some haughty explorer claimed to have discovered. One day he would take exception to the notion that Parcells was his mentor. Belichick had watched his father. He had watched Marchibroda, Shurmur, Glanville, Reese, Red Miller, lots of people. However, he would be linked to Parcells for many years. That link would gradually weaken in the late 1990s. It would pop, dramatically, at the end of 1999 and in the first few weeks of the new millennium.

But no one could have imagined that in '79, when New York Giants head coach Ray Perkins was looking for a special-teams coach. The foreshadowing was there, but who could see it? Who would guess that Adams, who also began working with the Giants in '79, would still be a key member of Belichick's football Cabinet? A sergeant's son,

Romeo Crennel, would arrive in New York two years after Belichick. Who would guess that he would one day become the top coordinator in the NFL as part of Belichick's staff?

There was one clue that the twenty-seven-year-old Belichick would be just as forceful as the fifty-year-old Belichick. He made it known in the beginning that he was a coach, not one of the guys. He looked young. He *was* young. He was in good shape from his days of playing football and lacrosse. It would have been easy for players to look at this assistant coach as a peer, not as someone charged with giving and teaching them assignments.

"It was an awkward relationship because in a lot of cases I was younger than the players," he says. "Each year I was older than a couple more guys. But for a lot of years there were a bunch of players, certainly the higher-profile guys, who were older than I was. You know, I was never one to go around with the players anyway. I could relate to them because I was their age, but I was never gonna hang out with them and do some of the shit that they did.

"And I knew it wasn't the right thing to do anyway. It would be great for a night, but in the long run it could really deteriorate your relationship. Everybody that I'd worked with told me that too. Ted told me, Rick told me, Red told me."

They told him because they knew there would be a point when he would be challenged. Some player was going to step up, and the young coach was going to have to prove that he was in authority. That happened in New York, and it happened during one of Belichick's first meetings in front of the entire team. He was trying to explain how the Giants were going to handle a technique when he noticed a conversation to his left. One of the players was laughing, trying to get the attention of his buddy. Belichick called the player out, and the player replied with a verbal jab of his own. Perkins was watching the exchange, but he didn't say anything. Belichick took over then.

"Shut the fuck up, all right? If you don't want to sit here, then just get the fuck out of here. But this is important. Everybody else is listening."

No more words were necessary. The talking and laughing stopped, and the new special-teams coach in New York was able to make his point. Perkins approached him afterward and told him the performance was great. It's what the head coach had wanted to see. Perkins was a tough coach who saw no problem with starters playing on special teams. When Belichick needed to be backed because players were late for special-teams meetings, Perkins was there to give him support.

"If they're late, you just have to fine 'em," he would say.

And it wasn't hard to figure out why some players were late. They didn't want to be there. Since the rosters were smaller in '79, special-teamers were closer to being starters then than they are now. There weren't as many players on teams then who were known purely as great "gunners," for example. They were backups in many cases, third receivers and third corners, who would have much rather been on the field for three downs than for one. They were among the first group to hear what Belichick tells all his players now. He tells them about the importance of teams, being attentive on teams, and being in position to turn the game on teams. He said it in '79. He said it in '02.

Appropriately, his words have always had a resounding economy to them. When he speaks to his team, no one is murky about where he stands. He has an opinion. It is always direct, and depending on the subject, it is sometimes rimmed with the obscene. He has been speaking to professional football audiences for more than half of his life. All he requires is for you to be alert, listen, and do what's supposed to be done. Trust him. There's an art to playing this game.

THE FOXBORO TRIANGLE: THE KRAFTS, PARCELLS, AND BELICHICK

It was a Tuesday morning, just after ten o'clock, when Bill Belichick was having a meeting with his trusted adviser and friend, Ernie Adams. They were exchanging ideas about the Tennessee Titans, whom they would play six days later in Nashville. Belichick and Adams were talking about ways to stop quarterback Steve McNair when they were interrupted by a soft knock on the office door.

A few seconds later a man who is also in the football business joined them. It was Robert Kraft. He was just stopping in to hear the experts analyze pro football, a sport he obsesses over as much as they do.

He listened to their comments on quarterbacks who can run. "We are so slow on defense,"

Belichick said, "that scrambles bother us a lot more than other teams. I'll bet Daunte Culpepper scrambled for more yards against us than he did anyone all year. Or close to it." Kraft listened to them talk about McNair—"You almost have to treat him like a running back"—and watched them dig into their archives for any plan of theirs that had once slowed the 235-pound quarterback. They came up with a New York Jets game plan from November 1998, when the Jets beat the Tennessee Oilers, 24–3. McNair was so bad that day that Dave Krieg replaced him. Expecting anything close to that same outcome was a reach, but at least they were holding proof that it could be done.

Kraft listened to them promise to fix an aspect of their defense: "We're going to get this 'mirror' straightened out if we don't do anything else this week." An effective mirror would put them in position to limit a quarterback's scrambling. Kraft listened to a few more minutes of planning before he quietly slid out the door.

Kraft, the team owner, would probably return later and listen to Belichick's thoughts. Or he might call from his office and try to understand a part of the game the way his head coach understood it. He knew he could talk to Belichick without any charges of being a meddlesome owner. And Belichick knew that when he was in conversations with Kraft he was talking to both a curious football fan and an exceptional businessman. Each man was receiving something—an implicit understanding between coach and owner—that had eluded him in the past.

After Bill Parcells left New England in 1997, Kraft and his family had to fight the perception that their constant hovering and tinkering had driven Parcells away to New York. On the September night Parcells returned to Foxboro with his new love, the Jets, a one-liner by former *Boston Globe* columnist Mike Barnicle captured a local sentiment that was gaining popularity. "I did not realize," Barnicle wrote, "that Amos Alonzo Kraft was the true architect of this team."

The reference to the football coaching legend and the suggestion that the owner was some type of intrusive football demigod annoyed Kraft, then and now. "Look, we're going to pay attention. I think fans should want owners who are going to pay attention," Robert Kraft says. "It's our financial net worth on the line. In Parcells, we had a guy who was coaching year to year. And the issue of his contract was supposed to be irrelevant to us? That's preposterous."

Too, the Krafts had dealt with Parcells every day. They knew how he had made them feel. Robert is careful and diplomatic when talking about Parcells today, but you can sense that there is a vast network of emotions lingering beneath each safe sentence. Jonathan Kraft, the team's vice chairman, is more candid on the subject. "I hated the man with a passion," he says. "He is someone who tried to make my father look bad. He tried to make him look foolish. And as a son, I hated him for it."

Belichick had arrived in New England as an assistant head coach during the height of Kraft-Parcells in 1996: "Obviously a lot of things had happened before I had gotten there. My sense of it was there wasn't a lot of communication." Once in New England, assistant coach Belichick and owner Kraft became friendly, and Belichick found himself much more comfortable speaking with him than he had been with Art Modell in Cleveland. They would converse several times a week, talking about football and the business of football. At times people overhearing their conversations would have thought, *Listen to these eggheads.*

There was the brainy Wesleyan graduate, with credentials in economics and Super Bowl defenses, talking with the multimillionaire Columbia University and Harvard Business School grad who had spent his entire forties and early fifties planning to buy the Patriots. And when Jonathan was part of their talks, another voice from Harvard Business School—via Williams College—was being heard. Belichick never found the discussions with Kraft to be taxing. "To me, what stood out was his smarts. He instinctively had good thoughts on football, and he understood why something would or would not be a good idea. Whereas Art had that same curiosity, and he had no idea of why things might be happening. None."

Kraft's thoughts on the game were so good because he had loved it and tried to live it since his youth in Brookline, Massachusetts. He graduated from Brookline High in 1959, one year before the Patriots were born. He was small, no more than five-foot-eight, but he always wanted to play. He knew it wasn't possible in high school. He had to attend Hebrew classes every day after school, and Brookline played its games on the Saturday Sabbath. When he arrived at Columbia on an academic scholarship, the urge to play hadn't left him. His parents didn't know it, but he played on an intramural football team at school. That is, they didn't know it at first. They found out after a game against Penn in which Robert injured his knee and needed surgery. Before operating, the school tried to contact the Krafts, but they didn't answer the phone until after sundown on the Sabbath. When representatives from Columbia finally got through, the news broke:

SCHOOL: "We need permission to operate on your son."
HARRY KRAFT: "What happened?"
SCHOOL: "He was hurt in today's game."
HARRY KRAFT: "What game? A football game? What?"

He was just a kid, not even twenty-one. But it was clear then that, somehow, football was going to be a part of his life. When he was twenty-nine and the father of a young family, he arrived at his Newton home and was greeted at the front door. That was part of the routine. The house at 60 Graylynn Road had a foyer on its right side, and that's where Kraft would meet his wife and sons. It was 1971, so his oldest, Jonathan, was seven years old.

"Come on, I want to show you something," he said to the boy.

He opened his briefcase and showed him season tickets for the Patriots, who were playing at a new stadium in Foxboro. Jonathan was excited, although the tickets had caused a household problem. Myra Kraft was not happy with her husband, and Jonathan could hear her raised voice—his bedroom was next to his parents'—as she asked Robert what exactly he was doing. The tickets were not a good investment for a family that had just begun to build its wealth.

Myra could have won her argument strictly on the performance of the team: it was bad. The team won 24 games and lost 46 between 1971 and 1975. The best thing about the games was the time Kraft was able to spend with his sons. He'd pick up roast beef sandwiches from Proviser's Deli on Commonwealth Avenue and drive to the stadium. He'd slip a $10 bill to one of the parking guys so he could get a good spot and avoid the postgame traffic gridlock.

Sometimes he would have rolls of toilet paper with him. That was the local tradition at Patriots games. When the team scored, the people up high would throw their rolls and watch them unfurl into the crowd.

It was fun, even if the teams were no good. Through the years the family grew, and so did its dreams. Kraft began his career with a paper products company, Rand-Whitney, which was owned by his father-in-law, philanthropist Jacob Hiatt. Kraft displayed a velvet business touch by the time he was in his midtwenties: he analyzed the stock market, hit for about $40,000, and made strong investments. By the early 1980s Kraft had gone beyond simply owning a business. By that time he had long since founded International Forest Products and amassed enough capital to acquire Rand-Whitney. Now he was looking for more than season tickets in section 217. He wanted to buy the team. He wanted the team to play in a stadium that was more appealing than the low-budget bowl that sat on a hill just off Route 1. He was a Boston kid who in his lifetime had seen frequent championships from the Celtics. He saw a couple of titles from the Bruins and none from the Red Sox, the most heartbreaking bridesmaids of all. What he had really wanted to see was the Patriots win a Super Bowl. That way, he could point to them and proudly say it was his team.

That's what troubled him when part of his dream came true. He already owned sorry Foxboro Stadium, the team that played in it, and the land that surrounded it. In January 1994 he bought the team from James Busch Orthwein for a then-record sum of nearly $200 million. But by 1996 he had not worked out a deal for a new stadium, and he didn't have a championship. It mystified him that the team could be on the verge of winning a Super Bowl—XXXI—

but that pursuit was running equal, or even secondary, to the imminent departure of Parcells. It bothered and hurt him that opinions were split on the departure and that, in some precincts, he received the blame. It was hard to find an emotion for what happened to his team after Parcells left and before Belichick arrived, because it happened so quickly. The play was poor, the drafts were bad, and the middle management was second-rate. It was upsetting to him because this was happening to the Patriots. And the Patriots, in heart and deed, were his team.

"My father—I think people have always, throughout his life, underestimated him," Jonathan says. "He didn't come from a lot financially, and he was always underestimated. You can look at his business career, either how he started International Forest Products or even our ownership of [Boston television station] Channel 7. He would be told that he didn't have the resources, or the smarts, or what-ever it was. People would think he was crazy. But he would see things, map them out in his head, and once he commit-ted, he'd stick with something. He'd be tenacious as hell and stick with it."

Toward the end of the 1996 season Robert Kraft began to realize that he might have to use his tenacity in an un-usual way. He might have to use it to clear up the contract issues of his own head coach. Kraft was hearing rumors that Parcells was looking to move on to another team, even though he was still under contract with the Patriots. If this was true, it was going to be a problem. As Kraft understood Parcells's contract, the options were limited: Parcells could coach the Patriots in 1997; he could leave coaching alto-gether for a year and then return in 1998; or he could accept a deal with another team in 1997, which would result in a compensation windfall for New England.

Clearly there was discomfort between Kraft and Parcells, and the discomfort became intensely personal. It may have begun as a simple personality clash, a predictable occupational hazard given the profiles of both men. Parcells, after all, was recognized as one of the best coaches in modern football history and an owner of things—championship rings—that Kraft coveted. His charisma was difficult to match too. Parcells's daily press conferences were reality TV shows before the term even existed. Members of the media would show up for updates from the solo character just to see what kind of colorful verbal frames he would place on ordinary football pictures. No one in the NFL was better at entertaining you for thirty minutes without revealing an ounce of substantive news. He'd waddle into the room, sit at a table, and begin with a familiar line, "Fire away, fellas." On the days he really had it going, Parcells would grant a backstage pass to the media members. After the press conference he'd chat for an additional ten, fifteen, sometimes twenty minutes. Parcells was good at detecting the pulse of the media, and he should have been: he demanded that clips from the New York and Boston newspapers be placed on his desk by seven A.M., and sports-talk radio was often the soundtrack in his office. He had a lot of caricature in him, the Jersey wiseguy who was always on the verge of telling you that he knew a lot more than you did.

Not only was Kraft a new owner, but he was an owner who had inherited Parcells's contract. The coach was actually signed by Orthwein, Kraft's predecessor. Orthwein stayed out of Parcells's way and let him run football operations as he saw fit. Kraft wasn't going to do that. He believed in giving managers their space, but he did not believe in giving any manager carte blanche. He wasn't going to let Parcells wall himself off in football operations while "the suits" did their jobs elsewhere. As an owner, he was going to ask business questions. And as a football fan who had paid more for a team than anyone before him, he believed he was entitled to have his football questions answered. It was his team.

There was no compatibility between the two. While Belichick and Kraft would talk for hours about the game as well as the mathematical principles that are applied to the salary cap–driven NFL, Kraft had no such bond with Parcells. In a way, the differences between Kraft and Parcells helped expose the growing differences between Belichick and Parcells. One man was uncomfortable with the owner's style. One man was eventually impressed by it. "Everyone has dreams, but the Krafts take it up a notch or three," Belichick once said. "Hey, a lot of people dream of meeting a rock star one day; Robert brings in Elton John for his anniversary party. When you and I receive a box or a package in the mail, we want to know what's inside. So does Robert, but before he gets to all that, he's figuring out whether he manufactured the box. And if not, why not? It's probably a different way of thinking from most people, but I think it's one of the things that draws us together."

Things didn't draw Kraft and Parcells together. People did. On January 12, 1997—the morning of the AFC Championship game—Will McDonough, the legendary *Boston Globe* columnist, approached the owner. McDonough was close to both Parcells and Kraft, and while McDonough believed that Kraft intentionally misled him prior to the NFL draft in April 1996, he knew he could still talk to him. They needed to talk. The *Boston Herald* had broken a story that explained why the Patriots would indeed be due compensation if another team wanted to hire Parcells. McDonough, also a reporter for NBC, had interviewed Parcells early on the morning of the 12th. Of course, Parcells had already read and reacted to the *Herald* article. He suspected that Kraft had given the story to reporter Kevin Mannix, and he was furious about it.

In recounting his version of the Kraft-Parcells relationship just over a month later in the *Globe*, McDonough wrote that he had wanted to talk with both men in January so that they could—temporarily at least—work together peacefully. "I told [Parcells], 'Listen, I'll grab Kraft when he gets here, bring him into your office, and straighten this thing out. He told me all along he wants to take the high road. Let's see what the deal is.'" Kraft remembers being surprised when McDonough approached him that day in '97. "Will said to me, 'I need to mediate something with you and Bill.' I said, 'What are you talking about?' He said something about Parcells wanting to get out of his contract. It felt like they were trying to browbeat me."

It was a lot of action, and the AFC Championship game still was four hours away. Once it started, the Patriots were in control against the Jacksonville Jaguars. They were 20–6 winners. Kraft, close to his three-year anniversary of ownership, was going to have a shot at a Super Bowl ring. He spoke on the field after the game, and no one could have guessed that there had been a problem with Parcells earlier in the day. He called the coach one of the NFL's greatest and said, "This is one of the great moments of my life. This is why our family got into the sports business. We have built something special here, and we owe it to the efforts of our players and our coaching staff. I can't even describe the feeling. I'm ecstatic. I'm happy. I'm content."

That feeling would last for a week. On January 20, a depressing Monday for Patriots fans, McDonough filed a stunning story from New Orleans. The message in the news story was as blunt as its headline: "Parcells to Leave." The major reason given for the decision, McDonough wrote, was a deteriorating relationship between Kraft and Parcells. Leaving was not going to be that simple for the coach, but it was probably best for him to leave anyway. He wasn't happy with the organization, and it wasn't happy with him. The season had been filled with bizarre messages, both overt and subtle, and this topped all of them. Each member of Parcells's coaching staff probably had his own threshold moment, a moment when he realized that the season was actually a nonfootball weekly drama.

"I don't know if I could really put my finger on it," Belichick says now of the '96 season. "I mean, there were times when things would look okay, and there were times when it would look hopeless. And yet, there could be some fluctuation in there. I think two events really stick out."

One was Terry Glenn. The rookie receiver didn't like to fly, especially when the weather was bad. He was uncomfortable flying with the team to New York and was looking for Parcells to talk to him about it. "So Charlie [Weis] brought him to me because he couldn't find Bill," Belichick says. "We couldn't find Bill because Bill had left. *He* didn't want to fly. And he wound up disciplining Terry for the same thing the head coach was doing. So it's hard to show consistency there."

The second event was Super Bowl XXXI. The Patriots were going to be facing the Green Bay Packers and league MVP Brett Favre. They were double-digit underdogs. But the intriguing stories were not about stopping Favre and blocking defensive lineman Reggie White. The Parcells story was the story.

"Yeah, I'd say it was a little bit of a distraction all the way around," Belichick says. "I can tell you firsthand, there was a lot of stuff going on prior to the game. I mean, him talking to other teams. He was trying to make up his mind about what he wanted to do. Which, honestly, I felt totally inappropriate. How many chances do you get to play for the Super Bowl? Tell them to get back to you in a couple of days. I'm not saying it was disrespectful to me, but it was in terms of the overall commitment to the team."

The Patriots were staying at the New Orleans Marriott. According to Parcells's telephone records, there wasn't a lot of long-distance restraint in the Big Easy. His bill showed dozens of itemized phone calls to Hempstead, New York, the administrative home of the New York Jets. Kraft had his suspicions about the Jets and was convinced that Parcells already had a deal in place with them. The phone calls to New York—which were either brazen or thoughtless, given that the Patriots could view all their employees' records—were proof that something unusual was happening.

"It was a very, very strange time," Jonathan says. "And when you're not an expert at this business—you know we were still very new to the business—it can be educational. Big Bill had kept us in the dark on a lot of things. He probably misled us on some things. And we didn't know how to go about questioning it."

Nothing could be done to save the relationship—if it could be called that—between Parcells and the Krafts. It was over. Even without the stories and distractions, it was going to be hard for the Patriots to defeat the Packers. With everything that happened leading up to the game, it didn't seem wise to anticipate a New England win. This was nothing like the conference championship, when Kraft and Parcells could argue before the game and compliment one another afterward. That game was in the wintry comfort of Foxboro, against a team, Jacksonville, that was coming off an upset of Denver at home.

In Louisiana the Patriots were facing a Green Bay team that had scored the most points in the league and had given up the fewest. The Packers were better. They won the game, 35–21. It was competitive the entire evening, but the championship was secured on a dynamic sequence in the third quarter. Kickoff returner Desmond Howard ran 99 yards through the New England special teams and wound up with the game's final touchdown. It was both punctuation and puncture.

Robert Kraft left New Orleans knowing that he wouldn't be picking up a ring. Jonathan left wondering about the step his family would take next. Belichick, the coaches, and the players left with the understanding that Parcells would be officially off the clock. "Not flying back after the Super Bowl kind of—it sent a message to the team that probably wasn't a good one," Belichick says. "It was clear there were big issues brewing." Given his relationship with Kraft, Belichick was an early candidate. The Patriots wanted to hire him, and everything they saw told them that they should have hired him. Belichick would have been the perfect choice for the Patriots in February 1997. How many examples did Robert and Jonathan need to convince them?

The team's defensive backs would come up to Robert, unsolicited, telling him how talented their position coach was. Kraft would press them for specifics, and they would shake their heads and answer, simply, that he had a knack for telling them what would happen before it happened. He was a good teacher, someone who could teach you the proper way to jam at the line without being overwhelmed yourself. He was a craftsman, deft with small touches that you didn't notice until you had seen someone else try the same thing with less care.

Robert remembered the conversations. He remembered Belichick talking about the new NFL that the 1994 collective bargaining agreement had created. Under the system, Belichick theorized, a smartly managed team would be able to compete for playoff positions and, ultimately, championships each season. Jonathan remembered their conversations outside of fitness centers on the road and the weight room at home. It would be five or six in the morning. "And we'd sit and we'd talk for an hour. And he just— he clearly got it. It was certainly different than talking to Bill Parcells and Pete Carroll. It was on another plane, another dimension."

And it was Belichick who would say of Robert, "He has outstanding business sense. In today's game it helps the coach so much to have a resource like that. By virtue of someone with a business mind like his being around us, it helps the coaches coach, helps people manage others, and that translates to results on the field."

But they didn't hire him. They couldn't. How do you experience what they had with Parcells and then hire someone who has known him and been associated with him for more than a decade? The question held no weight instinctively, because Belichick's candidacy felt right. Logically, though, they kept coming back to this: they had known Belichick for several months, and Belichick had known Parcells for several years.

There was also bitterness. Jets-Patriots was a nasty rivalry on its own. Now it had elements of Auburn-Alabama and Michigan–Ohio State. They were competing in the same division, for the same ring, with some of the same players and coaches. The Patriots would have to compete without Belichick. After the whir of compensation, hiring, and organizational reordering, this is how everything looked:

- Belichick and Parcells (along with Weis and Romeo Crennel) were in New York
- Former Jets coach Pete Carroll, who had been the defensive coordinator with the 49ers, was the new man in Foxboro
- Bobby Grier was in charge of New England's personnel department
- The Patriots, a young team fresh from a Super Bowl loss, were stocked with extra draft picks from a division rival.

The atmosphere may have seemed calm, but the Patriots had already begun declining. They didn't have unity in their management team, and that set the fractious tone for what would happen on the field. Carroll was a fine defensive coach, one who would eventually turn the University of Southern California program into one of the best in college football. But he was not the right hire for the Patriots. He was a nice man. He played the piano. He believed in the power of positive thinking and often talked about mind over matter. He was smart and decent. Yet his players could see the ceiling on his power. With Parcells, there was no compassion committee anywhere else in football operations. You had a problem? You dealt with him or you didn't play. In the new Patriot hierarchy, Grier found the players and Carroll coached them.

"I never heard people complain about his Xs and Os. I think people thought he actually knew the game of football," Jonathan says. "But beyond that, you know, as a manager of people—which is what a coach has to be too—he didn't know how to manage people. He would have been a good schoolteacher. He is a good teacher. A good teacher, not a good manager."

Carroll was the face of the post-Parcells Foxboro, even though he had just a fraction of Parcells's influence. He went 10–6 in his first season. He saved his job in his second year by going 9–7 and making the play-offs, despite a late-season injury to quarterback Drew Bledsoe. After Carroll went 8–8 in 1999, he lost his job, and so did Grier.

The organization was going to have to start over, but not over in the sense of the days before Robert Kraft. Technologically, the Krafts had an advanced organization. They had a vibrant website and a full-color weekly newspaper. They had good contracts—and contacts—with local television and radio stations. They were clever and conscientious marketers. They didn't have their new stadium yet, but they did have plans to build a privately financed facility for $325 million.

They also did not have the economist, the coach they should have hired in 1997. They knew they had to hire Belichick this time, and they knew they were the ones who were going to have to come up with the compensation. Coming up with the right package was just as difficult as talking about what the package would be; the Jets and Patriots were hostile neighbors. In the early stages of the talks to bring Belichick to New England, Steve Gutman of the Jets and Andy Wasynczuk of the Patriots did the negotiating. Jonathan Kraft was not going to speak to Parcells, and Robert talked with him only when the compensation package had been agreed to and approved by the league. Once they hired Belichick, the Krafts knew they could get what they had dreamed of back in 1988, when Robert Kraft outbid Victor Kiam by $6 million and plucked Foxboro Stadium out of bankruptcy court. Kiam had called the stadium a "pig" in '89, and he was probably right—aesthetically. But Kraft had outbid him because he knew the stadium was the key to Patriot survival: you couldn't, as Kiam did, buy the team without the stadium and do well. Kraft knew that when things were right, his organization would not have repulsive scandals, as it did in '86 and '90. He knew that one day a disappointing season would be defined strictly in football terms.

"This used to be a laughingstock," Jonathan says now in his stadium office. There is a flat-screen television turned to a financial channel. There are photos of recent exuberance just around the corner. In another room there is a Lombardi Trophy. "We had to prove to people you could give us your confidence, your trust, your money. No one ever wanted to invest confidence, passion, trust, time, money in the Patriots because they were going to be let down. Someone was going to do something stupid. The organization wasn't going to commit the resources. It wouldn't have been worth it. Well, we wanted to make it worth our resources to the general public. And that's what we did externally, and that's what we told our marketing department. And we said to the football side: 'We want to compete every year. How do we go about creating a system to do that?'"

In 2000 they knew the answers would lie in the hiring of Bill Belichick. If there was anyone who understood systems, how to apply them, and how to hire personnel to execute them, it was him. The fighting between the Jets and Patriots almost prevented it from happening. Robert Kraft was aware that he might need a backup plan if Belichick couldn't be released from his New York contract, so the owner traveled all the way to Palm Beach Country Club to secretly meet with an alternative candidate. He interviewed Butch Davis, who was then the head coach at the University of Miami. Davis intrigued him enough to earn a second interview. He took a private jet to Boston and checked into a hotel under an assumed name. The pursuit of Davis ended when the relationship between the Jets and Patriots softened enough to make a deal. The Patriots gave the Jets three draft choices, including a first-rounder in 2000, and the Jets freed the coach from his contract.

The twenty-four-day New England–New York episode was over. It had begun with Belichick scrawling his resignation on a piece of paper—he wrote that he was resigning as "HC of the NYJ"—and it had ended, technically, with the professional phone call between Kraft and Parcells. But it really wasn't over for anyone. The arguments, accusations, and stalemates had elicited emotions and thoughts that couldn't be easily reversed. Some relationships, like the one between Belichick and Parcells, would never be the same. Parcells would stay in the New York front office and Belichick would travel to New England and work for Kraft again. Soon Belichick would reconnect with old Patriots and introduce himself to new ones. He would shake hands, meet with heads of departments, and heads of businesses. There was an office in Foxboro waiting for him. He was going to need to fill that office with his football knowledge, his economic sensibility, and a symbolic hard hat. He had some rebuilding to do.

TOM BRADY AND THE RECONSTRUCTION

One of the best things about February 14, 2000, was the clarity it brought to Bill Belichick and his new employer, the New England Patriots. It was a switch from the first three weeks of the year, when nothing had been clear for either the coach or the organization. Belichick hadn't been sure if he could win his professional and psychological freedom from the New York Jets. Now that he had, he was rewarded with what could be best described as strange love.

It was Valentine's Day—Drew Bledsoe's birthday, ironically—and there was a piece of paper on the coach's desk spelling out the Patriots' depth chart in black and white. On this day the good news and bad news were the same for Belichick: this was his team now. It was exciting. And depressing. There had been hours of commentary on the public breakup of Bill Parcells and Belichick, but a larger point was often overlooked: the Patriots were terrible, in more ways than most people knew.

The roster was uneven, flecked with veterans too close to the end and young players who were never going to meet projections. The offensive line was made up of twenty-two-year-old Damien Woody and four players—Max Lane, Derrick Fletcher, Todd Rucci, and Zefross Moss—on their way out of the NFL. In 1996 and 1997 the team had received six additional draft picks as compensation for losing Parcells and running back Curtis Martin, who was signed by the Jets as a restricted free agent. Five of those six picks were wasted on below-average players who combined to play 129 NFL games. Just one of the picks, running back Robert Edwards, was a good player. But after rushing for 1,115 yards in his rookie season, Edwards completely tore three ligaments in his left knee and partially tore another during a rookie flag-football game—on the beach—as part of the Pro Bowl festivities in Hawaii. His victory was avoiding an amputation and being able to walk without a limp. He would return to football, but he wouldn't be as skilled.

A pattern of financial mismanagement had settled in at Foxboro as well: the team was more than $10 million over the salary cap. Suddenly the Patriots were developing the tag of other unfortunate franchises: they were overpaying for a lack of production (Lane, Rucci) and unwilling or unable to be creative as productive players (Martin, Tom Tupa, Otis Smith) went to the Jets. It was not surprising to Belichick that as he took the job two of his best players—Tedy Bruschi and Troy Brown—were unsigned.

TOM BRADY AND THE RECONSTRUCTION

As bad as the contract situation appeared to be, there was something worse. The Patriots were a divided team, a tiny nation of fiefdoms. That was true of the locker room, and it was true of the coach–general manager relationship. Pete Carroll and Bobby Grier did not present a united front, and the players knew it. If some of them couldn't get what they wanted from Carroll, they were not above turning to Grier to see what he thought. The Patriots lacked leadership and knew nothing of meritocracy. Theirs was a culture of entitlement and preferential treatment.

Given all of the Patriots' poor qualities, a matchmaker would have never recommended that they go on a date with Belichick. He took an economist's view of spending, and they did not. He believed that the scouting department should be run by one of his best friends, Scott Pioli, and he seemed unconcerned that a rift or power struggle might ever develop between them.

"Why would it?" he once said. "I can't do Scott's job and he can't do mine. We work perfectly together."

He believed in some of the principles of the Naval Academy, where one of the traditions is a classic teamwork exercise. The young midshipmen, or plebes, are required to climb the twenty-one-foot Herndon Monument after it's been covered with 200 pounds of lard. They are expected to work together to find a way to change a hat atop the oily monument. Once they do that, they shed plebe status and move up a class.

Belichick also was adamant about his teams being able to bridge any of their racial differences. He was a teenager in the mid-1960s, one decade after the Supreme Court's *Brown v. Board of Education* ruling. He remembered the tension between some white students at Annapolis High and some black students at Bates High. He saw a lot—certainly not all—of that uneasiness reduced when the high school on Chase Street in Annapolis fully embraced integration and, as a by-product, began producing stronger sports teams.

Individually, the Patriots had a handful of players who were ready for the commitment that Belichick was going to demand. But the coach knew what this team was collectively when he helped create game plans against it in New York. It wasn't his type of group, and he began to change that without even realizing it. He began to turn the franchise into a champion early in the spring when he gave quarterbacks coach Dick Rehbein a predraft assignment.

Belichick told Rehbein the Patriots were planning to select a quarterback who could grow into Bledsoe's backup. There were two players Belichick had in mind, and he told Rehbein to work out both of them. One of them, Tim Rattay, was in Lafayette, Louisiana. The other, Tom Brady, was in Ann Arbor, Michigan.

Rehbein went to Louisiana first. He was instantly impressed with what he saw. He told Belichick that the only thing he didn't like about the six-foot Rattay was that "he's a little short," but the ability was undeniable. Rattay played in a spread offense at Louisiana–Lafayette, and he averaged 386 passing yards per game for his college career. Rehbein guessed that, within a year, Rattay would be ready to be a number-two quarterback.

After his visit to the University of Michigan, Rehbein made another enthusiastic trip home. He liked the Brady kid too, and the kid knew it. When friends asked Brady if he was getting any interest from pro teams, he told them that the Patriots were one of his suitors. Rehbein described him as a winner, a leader with a good attitude. The quarterbacks coach told Belichick that if a decision had to be made between the two, he would give the edge to Brady. Belichick had studied the tapes and felt the same way.

On April 21, deep into the second day of their first draft with the Patriots, Belichick and Pioli looked at their board. They had already selected Dave Stachelski, Jeff Marriott, and Antwan Harris. Brady was available in the sixth round, at pick number 199, and Belichick stared at his name. "Brady shouldn't be there," he said. "He's too good."

He had meant that Brady was good in a relief sense— good enough to fill the role that they had envisioned for him as a backup. He wasn't thinking of the Brady who grew up admiring Steve Young and Joe Montana. He didn't think of how much joy Brady had for playing just about anything as a kid in San Mateo, California, where he lived in a neighborhood with sixty kids. One family had nine children in the house, and the folks across the street from the Bradys had six. All of the neighborhood kids would run about playing football, baseball, capture the flag, and hide and seek. Brady was energized by competition. He liked to talk about it, and he liked to be a part of it. When he wasn't throwing footballs with his right hand, he was trying to hit baseballs as a lefty, just like his favorite players—Wade Boggs, Don Mattingly, and Will Clark.

The Patriots took Brady at 199 and watched the 49ers take Rattay at 212. It was as if they got a quarterback and the lead foreman of their cleanup crew with one pick.

Brady would grow into Bledsoe's backup, as predicted. But he would quickly outgrow the job.

Before 2001 it had been eight years since Bill Belichick had had to make a tough quarterback call. Back then, in Cleveland, it wasn't just a choice of quarterbacks. It was perceived as a cultural statement. Bernie Kosar was one of them, a northeastern Ohioan who wanted to play for the local team. Belichick was seen as the cold outsider, the Browns' coach who could matter-of-factly say what the fans—and even owner Art Modell—didn't want to hear. He said that Kosar had "diminishing skills" and that was why he was released midway through the 1993 season.

"In the end, I just didn't really feel like it was going to work out," Belichick recalls. "Even though Vinny [Testaverde] was hurt, I knew he was coming back at some point. It was either deal with the problem or postpone the problem. So after we lost to Denver, Mike Lombardi and I talked to Art. We all sat in the office in the stadium and talked about it. I think we were all in agreement about what had to happen. And then the next day we had a staff meeting and talked about it again. Everybody was in agreement again."

So Kosar, from a town just sixty miles east of Cleveland, was loosed. It's hard to make a bolder move than that.

"I felt like it was the right thing to do. Here, more than ten years later, I think it's clear-cut from a football standpoint," Belichick says. "And I say that respectfully of Bernie, who did everything you would want a football player to do. He worked hard, was smart, understood the game—all those things. I just thought Vinny was a better player."

He thought Brady was better than Bledsoe in 2001 too. He had noticed Brady's leadership qualities during the previous year's rookie minicamp. If a group task needed to be done—if twenty-five guys needed to be organized—Brady was the one doing the organizing. His coach liked his approach, even when he was a fourth-stringer behind Michael Bishop. Brady often praised Bishop's arm strength, said he was one of the most talented athletes he'd ever seen, and did some self-scouting of his own. He could learn a lot from Bledsoe, John Friesz, and Bishop. Brady thought he must have been a fourth-string quarterback for good reasons, so more work needed to be done.

He took football seriously. He knew the playbook well and often imagined himself running the team. He developed a reputation as the hardest worker in the weight room, often causing strength coach Mike Woicik to say, "He works just as hard during the season as he does during the off-season program." Brady had a leading man's ability to hold the attention of the audience and a senator's flair for working the room. He would talk and listen to anyone, regardless of how different they were from him.

Brady kept pushing the people in front of him. He passed Bishop on the depth chart. At the end of the 2001 training camp he had passed veteran Damon Huard, who had been expected to be the team's number-two quarterback. Bledsoe did not have a good preseason, but it was going to be hard for Brady to pass him too. Bledsoe had just signed a ten-year, $103 million contract extension. He had become a familiar member of the greater Boston community and a favorite of the Krafts. But the coaches had noticed Brady's ascent, and Bledsoe's play early in the '01 season was making the twenty-four-year-old Brady difficult to ignore.

After losing their opener to the Bengals, the Patriots played the Jets on September 23 in Foxboro. It was one of Bledsoe's worst days as a pro. His numbers didn't dismay the coaches as much as his judgment did. He had a delay-of-game penalty after Belichick and offensive coordinator Charlie Weis had decided to go for a touchdown on fourth-and-goal from the 1. Four minutes apart in the first half, he had an intentional grounding penalty and an interception, both in New York territory. He was costing the team points and field position in what was obviously going to be a close game.

With five minutes remaining, Bledsoe's miserable play no longer was the day's central issue. On a third-down scramble from his 19, Bledsoe moved toward the right sideline. He gained 8 yards and was cleanly and ferociously hit by linebacker Mo Lewis. Bledsoe didn't know it then, but blood was beginning to leak into his chest cavity. An artery near his rib cage was partially torn, and he had what the team would call a sheared blood vessel. He returned to the game after the Lewis hit, but the pain had worsened. Brady took over in the final two minutes and drove the team to the New York 29 with fourteen seconds left. Four incomplete passes later, the Patriots had lost, 10–3.

Bledsoe spent four days in Massachusetts General Hospital. A tube was inserted in his chest to remove blood and cycle it back into his circulatory system. When he was sent home on the 27th, he was told he couldn't do any heavy lifting—carrying his young children included—for two weeks.

He could attend meetings and help Brady on the job, but he couldn't practice.

The Patriots won their first game, on the 30th, against the Colts. They lost the next week in Miami and then came home to beat the Chargers in overtime. They were 2–3, and all along Bledsoe thought Brady was temping in his place. He was wrong for several reasons. Brady was better than Bledsoe thought, and the organization was different from the one he had known for the past three seasons. Under Belichick, all Patriot jobs could be classified as temporary. They were earned and held by performance, not status or longevity. Belichick didn't go out of his way to antagonize stars, nor did he do anything special to accommodate them. He believed that one trait made all pro athletes equally created.

"We can talk about money, we can talk about trophies, talk about all that shit, okay? But the thing that means the most to players is to be able to go out there and get on the stage," Belichick says. "Once you take the stage away from them—whoever it is—they have nothing that can match it. You can talk about all the money they have in the bank, but if they don't have their self-esteem and their pride, then they don't have their stage."

After the Patriots lost to the Rams on November 18, Bledsoe wanted that stage back. He had been helpful in quarterback meetings and games, dispensing advice to Brady. Now his chest had healed and the doctors had cleared him to be on the field. He wanted to play. And Brady wanted to play. In the past those who were clearly not in his quarterbacking class had always backed up Bledsoe. Once upon a time a faction of New England fans had asked to see Bishop as the starter. It was a request any reasonable fan would like to forget, a low test score that should be mercifully struck from the record. Brady was different. He was a more composed quarterback than Bledsoe, although he lacked his arm strength, experience, and pedigree. There was a fight for a position that talent alone was not going to settle. A judge—in this case Belichick—was going to have to make a ruling.

"It's a competitive environment. I sure as hell didn't want to give up the job," Brady says. "Part of the reason I was ready then was that the year before I had prepared like I was going to play. I was confident, and the coaches were confident in what I could do."

For the fans, Bledsoe versus Brady had turned into Nixon versus Kennedy, circa 1960. It was the major topic on sports radio stations and the question with which the sports pages grappled. There was no predictable chart or grid for Bledsoe or Brady supporters: some husbands liked Bledsoe and some wives liked Brady; some brothers liked Brady and some sisters liked Bledsoe.

This wasn't necessarily Belichick's repeat of the Cleveland Kosar-Testaverde controversy. He wasn't going to have to cut a popular player. But he was in his second year, rattling a star who had spent nine years as the franchise's best-paid and most marketed athlete. Belichick's choice meant that he would have the most talented and most expensive backup quarterback in the NFL. Making the decision would not be a problem. Presenting that decision would turn the situation into an awkward and eventually nasty one. When Belichick did not return the job to Bledsoe or give him an opportunity to win it back with practice reps, Bledsoe interpreted that as the coach lying to him. The charge irked Belichick.

"I don't feel like I misled him. I really don't. You know, that kind of bothered me. I understood his disappointment, I understood he wanted to play, I understood that he was a good competitor. He was a hardworking guy, he had been in the organization a long time, and I respected that. Nobody wanted him to get hurt and miss two months. There was nothing we could do about it. You don't take a player who hasn't played in two months and then just stick him back in there like nothing had happened."

It was too late. Bledsoe felt that he had been deceived. Belichick says that he offered Bledsoe the chance to get something back, all right: timing, not a job. "I wasn't talking about him as a starter. I was talking about him at least throwing to guys that he might be throwing to in the game, if he had to play as a backup. Which ultimately happened in the AFC Championship game."

It was a long road to Pittsburgh, though. With the unexpected death of Rehbein in the summer of 2001, Belichick had become the quarterbacks coach. He often met with Brady, Bledsoe, and Huard in a small Foxboro Stadium office. It was uncomfortable in there, and not just because the stadium was outdated.

"I knew he was unhappy," Brady says of Bledsoe. "It was strained. When Coach Belichick was around, Drew would become quiet and reserved." Bledsoe was the same way in the team captains' meetings on Tuesday nights. The meetings were designed so that there could be an exchange between the coaching staff and the players. But the meetings were inadequate for Belichick-Bledsoe. The other captains noticed it and occasionally commented. One of the captains was Bryan Cox, the inimitable linebacker who always carried an extra opinion just in case you didn't have one of your own. He had also lost his job to injury, but didn't respond the way Bledsoe did. Of course, Cox brought that up once or twice in the captains' meetings.

"You could feel the strain in the relationship all the way around," Belichick says. "I mean, I met with the quarterbacks every day: myself, Drew, the other two quarterbacks, and Charlie. There is no question that there was discomfort in the room."

Outside of the team, Bledsoe's urban legend began to grow. The popular story was that the quarterback was the opposite of the modern athlete and that he *didn't* let his agenda interfere with the overall mission of the team. It wasn't quite that clean. Bledsoe wasn't reckless in the office, but it was known how angry he was. He had his problems with Belichick, but he also wasn't happy with Weis. He did have an outlet for his anger: Woicik's and Markus Paul's weight room. In there he became tougher and pushed himself harder than he ever had. Woicik and Paul didn't find fault with his work habits and attitude. But this was Bledsoe-Brady, where no judgment was unanimous.

During a staff meeting one of the coaches said of Bledsoe, "His shitty attitude means we have to do one of two things: trade him to the highest bidder [in the off-season] or tell him he's the starter and Brady will compete with him."

Brady says Bledsoe was professional with him and never focused on the situation at work. "But it was definitely hard on our personal relationship. Drew and I were friendly, but we were already very different. I was twenty-four and he was twenty-nine. He had a family and I was single. Lots of things. We were never really great social friends."

They had a decent working relationship, good enough for the team to make it to the Super Bowl. On the way there, in the AFC Championship game on January 27, 2002, against the Pittsburgh Steelers, Brady sprained his left ankle in the second quarter and was replaced by Bledsoe. The veteran excitedly ran on the field and began whipping passes. He threw a touchdown pass to David Patten and made two difficult completions to Brown and fullback Marc Edwards. He completed 10 of his 21 passes that day for 102 yards. When it was over, he cried.

As emotional as the Pittsburgh game was—Bledsoe received a game ball—the quarterback was still being evaluated. According to the coaches' game breakdowns, Bledsoe's statistics were: one mental error, four bad throws, and four bad choices. The logical counterargument to those unflattering numbers was rust. How could Bledsoe expect to play well when the majority of his reps hadn't come with the starters? How could he be sharp when he hadn't played in a game in four months?

Belichick didn't view it that way. As much as he respected Bledsoe, he had an idea of what his quarterback should do. The model for that idea was Brady. Brady had shown an ability to stay calm, recognize defensive nuances, and shout out the necessary adjustments for his receivers, backs, and linemen. When he coached against Bledsoe in New York, Belichick would often present the quarterback with a "Cover 5" defense. It features man-to-man coverage with two deep safeties to help on the receivers. Belichick would tell his defensive backs to be physical at the line of scrimmage. Then he would play the educated odds, going with scientific and anecdotal research that revealed Bledsoe would not be accurate enough or patient enough to make the throws that could defeat an effective "Cover 5."

It didn't take nearly as much research to figure out Bledsoe's post–Super Bowl stance. After New England won the first Super Bowl in its history, Bledsoe did not respond to the Patriots' calls or letters when the team was attempting to coordinate an off-season workout schedule.

"It was clear to me he didn't want to be on this football team," Belichick says. "And in the end I had to decide whether to resolve the situation before training camp. It was clear to me at that point that there would be some kind of confrontation one way or the other. He was starting to take a stand."

The stand was probably good for everyone. It made the separation easier. Belichick could be unconventional at times, but he wasn't likely to bench a young quarterback who was MVP of the Super Bowl. Bledsoe would be able to leave New England knowing that he had rarely said or done anything that embarrassed the organization. The Patriots' reconstruction had begun to take shape soon after Bledsoe's twenty-eighth birthday. Now, with Bledsoe at thirty, it was time for some paperwork and other formalities to make the makeover complete.

Cincinnati called with a proposal. So did Buffalo. The Bills and team president Tom Donahoe were reluctant to give up a first-round choice for the quarterback. But when the Patriots didn't budge from their request on April 19, the day before the 2002 draft, Donahoe sent a fax to Foxboro. In it he said he was making his final offer, but any good negotiator could see through the claim. The fax was sent to

Belichick, Pioli, Robert Kraft, and chief operating officer Andy Wasynczuk. It was received at 11:47 A.M.:

> *Dear Scott,*
>
> *We realize how busy you, Coach Belichick, and your entire organization are in your draft preparations. We wish you good success this weekend with your picks.*
>
> *The Bills wanted to make one last attempt to complete a trade for Drew Bledsoe and wanted to state our proposal in writing so there is no confusion or miscommunication. If something is capable of being completed, we would like to know today. We feel that tomorrow everyone's focus needs to be on the draft.*
>
> ***PROPOSAL***
>
> *In the 2003 draft, the Bills will trade a solid #2 pick to New England for Drew Bledsoe. If Drew Bledsoe starts 12 games and the Bills go to the play-offs, the pick becomes the Bills' #1 pick in 2003. However, if Bledsoe fails to report and/or pass a physical, the trade becomes null and void.*
>
> *After you have a chance to discuss our proposal, please give Jim Overdorf or myself a call to discuss further. Thank you and all the best this weekend.*

Two days later Bledsoe was in Buffalo. The cost for Donahoe and the Bills was a first-round pick, regardless of Bledsoe's or the team's performance. In Buffalo, Bledsoe would get the chance to start again. He would be going to a team with two good receivers in Eric Moulds and Peerless Price, a good running back in Travis Henry, and an offensive coordinator, Kevin Gilbride, who would give the quarterback an opportunity to take several "shots" down field every game. He also would have a chance to play the Patriots twice a year.

The Patriots had what they wanted. To them, Brady was more than a quarterback who watched ESPN and said to himself, "I never want to be on that crawl at the bottom of the screen: 'Patriots quarterback Tom Brady arrested. . . .' I never want to look like an ass who will let down my family, my teammates, and my organization." He was more than a connoisseur of competition, one who would watch professional and amateur runners in the Boston Marathon and exclaim, "These are some of the toughest people I've ever seen in my life." He was more than a man who was in awe of great writers, filmmakers, musicians, and even politicians. "Take the president of the United States, for example," he says. "I'm not talking about George Bush specifically as much as I'm talking generally about the position of president. What an awesome responsibility that must be, to lead a country under the most intense scrutiny." He was more than the leader who could speak warmly of taking hits: "The first game of the season, your jaw is aching, your head hurts, your hip hurts. As the season wears on, by week thirteen or fourteen, every single person in the league is hurt. You're limping to the bathroom in the morning."

For the Patriots, Tom Brady was the fictional character they put on paper and watched come to life. That's truly what happened. Pioli and Ernie Adams rewrote the scouting manual long before the team drafted Brady. If you read the Patriots' manual on the characteristics of a perfect quarterback, it's a Brady outline. It may not capture all the qualities of the real thing, but it comes close. As Brady carried the team closer to where it wanted to be, from a six-game winning streak at the end of the 2001 season to a win in the snow in a divisional play-off against Oakland, the manual began to read like the quarterback's biography. He was everything the Patriots wanted. "A quarterback for the New England Patriots must make the right decisions and make them fast," reads part of the manual. "Just because a person is smart does not necessarily mean they can make quick decisions under pressure."

On a February evening in New Orleans a smart Brady would make quick decisions under pressure. A worldwide audience would learn what the late Rehbein had seen in 2000. Brady was a team player. He would drive his team as far as he could as quickly as he could. And when he couldn't go any farther, he was confident that a kicker could finish the job.

DISSECTING THE GREATEST SHOW ON TURF

The smoky hotel room was not going to work for Adam Vinatieri. He knew it as soon as he opened the door marked 209. He was that rare business traveler in New Orleans, one who wasn't looking for a good time on a Saturday night. He didn't want to enter this room at the New Orleans Airport Hilton and be reminded of other places in the city. This smelled like a juke joint or pool hall, ventilation thick enough to alter one of his kicks.

He and his teammates had come here, thirteen miles away from the French Quarter, for a Saturday night of peace. Their previous hotel, the Fairmont, had been on Baronne Street. When you stayed there, you understood that temptation was as close as the next open window or elevator ride. There were Super Bowl crowds mixing with Mardi

Gras crowds. There were parades, clowns, and streakers. There were flashers, hustlers, and autograph seekers. The parties were plentiful, even if they were taking place during one of the most reflective periods in U.S. history.

On the first Saturday of February 2002, patriotism was running high and the country was at war. It was still difficult to grasp the totality of September 11, 2001, and the worst foreign attacks ever on U.S. soil. The Secret Service and forty-seven other local and federal agencies came to New Orleans, concerned that there might be another terrorist attack. The Louisiana Superdome was surrounded by cement barriers and chain-link fences and protected by snipers and fighter jets.

There was the poignancy of a team in red, white, and blue uniforms—called the Patriots no less—attempting to reach an ideal that has long resonated in the American soul. Here was the little guy trying to stop the machine, in this case the quick- and high-scoring St. Louis Rams. Here was the modest Main Street bodega trying to keep up with the corporate strip-mall chain. And here was someone holding one of the most marginalized positions in the game—kicker—trying to be sure he was as prepared as the quarterbacks, linebackers, and coaches.

Since he would kick off a party to be televised to the world the next night, and since he was already seeking perfection on Saturday to ensure that Sunday would be just right, he switched rooms. Vinatieri had a routine for everything. This had to be a part of it. Handling the small things now would make tomorrow seem more manageable. He would change rooms. He would attend the mandatory team dinner at 6:00. He would attend the mandatory squad meeting at 8:30. Then he would return to the clean air of his new room and slowly begin to focus on a game that he wasn't expected to decide. After the squad meeting, he was in for the night. He paged through some magazines, briefly listened to some television noise, and was in bed when one of the assistant coaches, Ivan Fears, began curfew checks after 11:00.

America hadn't laughed much in the months preceding the game, but America would have found this to be hilarious. This was the kicker? A *kicker* insisting on the proper environment? How was a kicker going to save the Patriots from the St. Louis Rams? How was perfection itself going to save these 14-point underdogs?

The Rams weren't just a football team; they were representatives of a culture that wants results and wants them quickly. They were as fast as the Internet, an instant-message offense. They had a three-season body of work that couldn't be matched by any offense in NFL history: 526 points in 1999 when they won Super Bowl XXXIV, 540 in 2000 when they made the play-offs despite being betrayed by their defense, and 503 in 2001 when they were starting to think of themselves as a young dynasty. Theirs was a powerful offense of illusion, one in which one play would appear to mirror the other. But there was always a blur in the mirror, a subtle motion that would play tricks with the reflection. It was one thing for opposing coaches to study the offense and figure out its complexities. It was something entirely different to take that message to their players and convince them, essentially, to disbelieve reality. Because, you know, the reality they thought they saw actually wasn't real.

It was too heady for most teams to comprehend. The 2001 Rams were computer-generated, with a carnival nickname—"The Greatest Show on Turf"—to match. Kurt Warner was the quarterback, and he was the league's MVP. Marshall Faulk was the running back, and he was the league's Offensive Player of the Year. Torry Holt and Isaac Bruce, the starting receivers, had combined to average 15 touchdowns per season since '99. The head coach was Mike Martz, a professorial Californian who was fascinated with the idea of making less look like more. And with all the attention given to pro football's number-one offense, it was easy to forget that the speedy St. Louis defense was ranked third in the league.

Martz, a Civil War scholar, gave a glimpse of his offensive philosophy a few days before the Super Bowl. "The Union Army was convinced that the Confederacy was twice the size it actually was," he told the *Detroit News*. "A lot of it had to do with the movement of the troops and where they were attacking. Deception is certainly some of what we do. It keeps people back on their heels and gives us probably a little more credit for what we are."

The deception had worked in November in Foxboro. The Rams played the Patriots in a regular-season game and won, 24–17. Warner passed for 401 yards, and the Rams' offense had twice as many yards as the Patriots'. If St. Louis could do that in chilly New England on slow grass, what would happen when the Rams were expected to be scientists in ideal laboratory conditions: domed stadium, 72 degrees, artificial turf?

Most football observers considered it to be a rhetorical question—yet they couldn't resist answering it anyway. From sportswriters to broadcasters to former coaches and players to celebrities to political talking heads, the opinions were nearly unanimous.

Marv Levy, former coach of the Buffalo Bills: "You have to pick the Rams. They're the most talented team I've seen in years."

Peter Brown of *The Sporting News*: "It's gonna be ugly. Cinderella eventually becomes a pumpkin. You can't be lucky and win the Super Bowl."

There were some exceptions, and a couple of them were surprising. One came from national security adviser Condoleezza Rice, a football enthusiast who dreams of being NFL commissioner. During an interview on CNN with Wolf Blitzer, Rice briefly changed the course of her conversation—she had been talking about terrorism—and gave an opinion on her favorite sport.

BLITZER: "So you want to tell us who's going to win the Super Bowl?"

RICE: "Well, shouldn't I be reserved if I'd like to eventually be commissioner? Let me just say this: if New England can stay in the game until the fourth quarter, I think they've got a very good chance to win this game."

One of the most ironic picks came from Cleveland, where the sideline star of the Patriots, Belichick, began his head coaching career. Five years after Modell had fired Belichick, New England was seeing what Cleveland expected in the early 1990s. An entire six-state region believed Belichick to be a football draftsman, capable of charting game plans so original that no team—the superior Rams included—would be able to separate the Patriots from their first championship. That was not the popular opinion in Cleveland. For many reasons, readers of the *Cleveland Plain Dealer* must have been stunned when columnist Bill Livingston predicted a Patriot win and explained it by writing, "Nobody can beat the Rams? I beg to differ. The Rams can. The only people who turn it over as much as the Rams are cooks at IHOP."

But St. Louis turnovers—and there were 44 of them during the season—would not guarantee a New England win. Belichick had said, with no trace of sarcasm, that his kicker was his most consistent player all season. That's usually not a good thing. But Vinatieri was different. Two weeks before the Super Bowl, Vinatieri had made a 45-yard field goal in a snowstorm to force overtime in a divisional play-off. He returned to win that game, against the Oakland Raiders, with a 23-yarder. He gained the respect of strength coach Mike Woicik by becoming stronger during the season. At one point Woicik said that Vinatieri had no physical weaknesses. He gained the respect of special-teams coach Brad Seely by kicking well in bad weather. He was a football player who happened to be a kicker, and his teammates accepted him as one of them.

Belichick liked the kicker too. But the coach and his staff were going to have to come up with something that relied more on art than sentiment to stop the Rams. When Belichick checked into his room at the Hilton, he found a foot-long, stuffed Rams doll lying on his bed. It was wearing a helmet, with pins stuck in its torso. Belichick wasn't sure who placed the effigy in his room, but he laughed and put the doll with his luggage. It was the Saturday before a game that could earn him a ring as well as redemption. He had already constructed a plan that could pierce the Rams. He had already announced to his team that the defensive plan from November—blitz!—was inadequate and that was his fault. He realized Warner's release was quick enough to make pressure negligible. The more the Patriots blitzed, the more space they created for him to throw, either in the seams or on the perimeter. A smart quarterback could sit back and fill the open spaces.

This time the strategy would have more thought. Martz appreciated military strategy from an academic point of view, but it was a way of life for Belichick and his defensive coordinator, Romeo Crennel. Belichick grew up in Annapolis, Maryland; an only child, his playground was often the U.S. Naval Academy campus where his dad worked. Crennel spent much of his childhood less than two hundred miles away in Lynchburg, Virginia, as his father went on assignments in Korea and Japan. Sergeant Joseph Crennel was in the Army for twenty-six years. He would give his five children household chores to do and then review them with a military inspection. One of his two boys, Romeo, planned to follow him as an enlisted officer. But when Romeo tried to get into the advanced ROTC corps as an undergraduate at Western Kentucky, he was denied; he was told he was overweight and had flat feet.

Both Belichick and Crennel had grown up with fathers who had minds for strategy and mothers who were gifted communicators. Mary Crennel was the perfect complement to Joseph. She believed in details too, but her approach was softer than the sergeant's. To win, the Patriots were going to need both: get the right plan and then present it to the team clearly and simply. Belichick and Crennel began talking about it after the AFC Championship game, on the plane from Pittsburgh to Boston. The next day, Monday, January 28, Belichick boarded a noon flight to New Orleans while Crennel and the other assistant coaches remained in

Foxboro. They studied tape of all the Rams games and followed their head coach to Louisiana on Tuesday afternoon.

Once he arrived at the Fairmont, Belichick faxed some ideas back home to Crennel. He also huddled with Ernie Adams, his old prep school buddy. Adams had a vague title with the Patriots—football research director—and could often be seen carrying either the *New York Times* or some four-hundred-page book. At Phillips Academy, Adams was so proficient in Latin that the school ran out of courses to offer him. He loved football too and was one of the few people who knew the name "Belichick" before Bill arrived on campus in the fall of 1970. Adams had already read Steve Belichick's book on scouting, *Football Scouting Methods*, and was eager to meet the author's son. Belichick and Adams played next to each other on the football team, center and guard, and they didn't venture far from each other—philosophically at least—after that.

While Adams was not a coach, Belichick consulted with him the same way a president consults with a top adviser. Once, during a training camp skit, Patriots rookies flashed a picture of Adams with the teasing caption, "Do You Know Who This Man Is?" It got a lot of laughs. No one could quite define Adams, but Belichick knew he was brilliant and could help him see things that might escape even some trained football eyes.

Crennel, Adams, and Belichick all came up with independent thoughts on defending the Rams. Belichick likes to see what his employees think, independent of him. "That way you don't have those crude masturbation activities. Sometimes somebody can get going and then everyone follows that line of thinking, that process. And then everybody agrees. It's better when we just analyze independently and all agree or work it out ourselves." Early on Tuesday they merged their brightest ideas and began to strip away some of the St. Louis mythology.

"They have five basic passing concepts," Belichick told Crennel later that day. "They don't have thousands of plays. If we stop those five concepts, we're going to have a chance. They change formations around, and they shift everybody all over the place. But if we can stop the concepts, that's the heart of what they want to try to do."

Belichick was a curious mechanic with the St. Louis offense in his hands. He had deconstructed the engine, tagged the most indispensable parts, and rearranged the structure just as he found it. Among the five concepts, he noticed that one truth rose above the other four: Warner, despite throwing for 4,830 yards (second-most in NFL history), was not the key to the St. Louis offense. Accepted NFL theory says that harassing the quarterback leads to mistakes. Belichick believed that, but with a twist. He planned to harass Warner by disrupting the most important player on the field.

Faulk.

The central concept of the plan was to annoy the running back, not the quarterback. Crennel, Adams, and Belichick had all seen the same things on tape. Within the shifting and motioning there were trends.

"If Marshall is in a 'home' position, we're not going to let him run the ball, okay?" Belichick said. "If he's in an offset position, we're not going to let the fucker release out in the backfield and catch the ball because we know we can't cover that. So the best time to get him is to get him on his way out. Our ends, instead of having them rush the quarterback, they should come off and hit Faulk. And then rush.

"We're not going to blitz Warner. We're going to force him to hold the ball and go to a secondary receiver."

The home position was Faulk's traditional place, lined up behind Warner. The offset position was when he was somewhere else, in position to run, take a screen, or run routes like a receiver. The entire offense made more sense when the actions of Faulk were studied.

That was half of the test. But there was still the issue of coaching the concepts and getting the players to play off them. With the game plan in their hands on Wednesday, the Patriot defense was told to concentrate on Ram generalities rather than specific shifts and motions.

- Watch Faulk.
- Be wary of Bruce in the slot, because he doesn't go there often.
- Don't ever make the mistake of thinking Faulk is staying home to block; that's either a screen or he's going to have a delayed release out of the backfield.
- The St. Louis tackles and guards often tip when they're setting up a screen—the tackles line up deep—and everyone on defense should recognize it.
- Remember, no matter what your eyes tell you, you'll never see the same play twice. It may look like the same play, but it's not. Don't play the actual play. Play whatever your assigned concept is.

- Be physical with them at all times. They don't like
  that.

"We're not going to say 'Watch out for these fifty things.'
It's too overwhelming," Belichick said. "The concepts will
get it done the majority of the time, as long as we don't give
up the big play. Hey, they're going to gain 10 yards anyway.
So if we say 'When Marshall's at home, play run,' and they
hit an out for 10, okay. Life goes on. Let's take away something and then we'll try to scramble to handle the things
that we know we're not quite as solid on."

The defensive theses began to be drilled on Wednesday
and Thursday mornings at 9:30, Friday morning at 8:30,
and Saturday morning at 9:00. You didn't have to glance at
the itinerary to know that there was a meeting, practice, or
treatment that you should be attending on one of those
days. Chances were that if you found yourself with a lot of
extra time, it meant you probably weren't where you were
supposed to be. The itinerary was so focused and detailed
that even the time to shower after practice—4:00 to 4:30—
was factored in.

Everyone knew what he was supposed to do. The receivers knew they had to run sharper routes than they had
in November. There could be no turnovers by the offense,
which gave the ball away three times in the first game, once
at the St. Louis 2-yard line. The kickoff coverage and return teams understood that they had to be better than they
had been two and a half months earlier.

By Saturday evening, their game plan memorized, Patriots players and staff found several ways to occupy themselves until Sunday.

Belichick had spent thirty minutes talking with two college friends, Mark Fredland and Jim Farrell, the three of them reminiscing about their alma mater, Wesleyan University in Connecticut. They barely mentioned football. Across town, team owner Robert Kraft was hosting a dinner at the Windsor Court Hotel. Jerry Jones, Bob Tisch, Lamar Hunt, and Al Lerner were among his guests. Following the dinner, Kraft headed to a Bourbon Street bar with his wife, Myra, and a couple of their friends. They stayed out until one A.M. with hundreds of Patriots fans who were so comfortable with the celebrity among them that they called the owner "Bobby," patted him on the back, and offered to buy him drinks. Kraft's eldest son, Jonathan, was in a casino with vice president of marketing Lou Imbriano. Jonathan watched Imbriano have one good roll and decided that was his cue to leave. "I don't want to affect the karma of tomorrow," he said as he went back to his hotel.

At the Airport Hilton, Tom Brady was telling himself how uncomplicated his quarterbacking was going to be the next day: "All I have to do is recognize the coverage, make sure guys are lined up right, read my progressions, and make the throw." And after getting himself into a non-smoking room, Vinatieri was having no problems. He was ready for tomorrow. He knew an early bus would leave the Hilton for the Superdome at 1:30 Sunday afternoon. He knew he was going to be on that bus.

PATRIOT REIGN

On the morning of Super Bowl XXXVI, Belichick had no remarkable speeches for the team. He gave the Patriots the major points of the plan once again, guessing it was the twentieth time they had heard these instructions from him.

He spent most of his time warning the players about the length of the day: it was going to be two hours longer than normal. He emphasized that the players needed to pace themselves. There would be long gaps between pregame warm-ups and introductions and another gap at halftime. The point was that they shouldn't expend too much too soon.

Belichick was thorough—as usual. At least he knew no one could ever use lack of preparation as an excuse. He thought of everything before games: weather, time-zone changes, officials, field quirks, unseen distractions. He was comfortable with his players and staff members taking different paths to readiness, as long as they were ready to do their jobs.

It was clear that he was the leader of an unusual group. They were diverse when it came to religion, age, economic status, philosophy, and race. But the uniting link began with football. They were one when they needed to be—on the field—and allowed each other space and individuality when they weren't playing.

That's why no one found it strange that assistant strength coach Markus Paul was reading the Bible on the way to the game as a few players sitting near him listened to hip-hop with explicit lyrics. They respected his interests—he was planning to read the Bible from start to finish—and he respected theirs. The players were even used to a smiling Paul telling them on Mondays, their muscles still sore from the game, why God was with them even as they lifted weights through the pain: "Come on and lift. You know He wouldn't put you in a situation that's too tough for you."

The entire team had arrived at the 72,000-seat Dome on Poydras Street by 3:00. They had looked out the bus windows to see thousands of fans already lined up for extensive security checks. It didn't take the players long to change into their uniforms and test the turf. Some guys saw players they knew and talked with them. Outside linebackers coach Rob Ryan looked across the field and saw Rams cornerback Aeneas Williams. Ryan was defensive backs coach in Arizona in 1994, and Williams had been his best player there, a corner whose Hall of Fame skills were on display in the NFL's literal and figurative desert. The

Cardinals, who have just a single play-off win since 1985, couldn't have dreamed of playing on the last Sunday of the year. Both men acknowledged how fortunate they were to be one win away from the oasis.

"Great thing is," Ryan said to Williams, "one of us is finally going to be a champion tonight." They laughed, both thinking that the other would leave Louisiana disappointed. Their last year together in Arizona, 1995, they were watched by 380,000 fans the whole season. Soon their game would be televised to nearly one billion people.

Pop star Mariah Carey was in the building to sing the national anthem. U2, Paul McCartney, and the Boston Pops were also there to perform. One of Belichick's heroes from Navy, Roger Staubach, was an honorary captain. There were stars on the field and in the stands. But moments before kickoff, fans in the stadium and those at home or at their local bars and pubs were struck by something else. One of the player perks of the Super Bowl is being introduced individually. It's not that each player is going to receive his fifteen minutes of fame, but for many unknowns—their anonymity doubled by wearing helmets—five to ten seconds of worldwide face time is an electronic souvenir, a natural TiVo moment.

But the Patriots chose to do something that was normal for them and inspiring to an audience that was seeing it for the first time. They chose to be introduced as a team. Forget about the individual announcements. They bounced out of their tunnel, a confident and unified mass of red, white, and blue. Four thousand miles away in Hawaii, Christian Fauria of the Seattle Seahawks watched the group introduction on TV and knew something extraordinary was going to happen in New Orleans. He called his father-in-law—they had a bet—and conceded defeat. The Seahawks' tight end had picked against the Patriots. He now understood that they were going to win.

"You've already won!" Fauria told his father-in-law. Then he talked to himself: "This is what football is all about. It's the biggest spectacle in sports and you give up your individual right to be noticed? The pinnacle of your career and you share it with some slapdick who is never going to see the field? It's commendable. It's, it's . . . man, I've got goose bumps."

At the start of the game, with camcorders and digital cameras tracking Vinatieri's kick to the St. Louis 1, the Patriots had a minor slip. They had spent considerable time on concepts to defend the Rams, but certainly not at the expense of anything else. With his experience as a special-teams coach with the Giants, Belichick often said he didn't understand why those coaches aren't considered more strongly for head-coaching jobs. Owners and general managers instinctively look to the coordinators, who are each in control of one-third of the game. Why not consider those in charge of the other third? Belichick's emphasis on teams was obvious. So he wasn't pleased when the Rams' Yo Murphy took the opening kick at the 1 and returned it 38 yards, the ball tickling the St. Louis 40-yard line.

Great, he thought. *They begin with good field position.*

Nine seconds later Warner connected with Holt for an 18-yard completion. Just like that, the Rams were at the New England 43. But the early drive, hurt by an offensive pass interference penalty, stalled.

There is so much analysis of the game, from obvious points of interest to minutiae, that the analysis itself can become an opponent during Super Bowl Week. One reason

Belichick wanted Brady to have the ball was that the quarterback had an equal understanding of primary and peripheral issues. After Brady called his first play—"O Flood Slot 74 Shout Tosser"—he was amazed at how natural the game felt. The play, which began at the Patriots' 3, was a 21-yard slant to Troy Brown. This didn't seem different from any other slant he had thrown his best receiver's way.

This is what the hype is all about? he said to himself, almost wanting to laugh. *It's a normal game.*

This coming from a guy who had been a fourth-stringer the previous season. He played as if he remembered that, and unlike many at twenty-four years old, he took few things for granted. His salary was $298,000, and he approached every football moment as if that salary were on the verge of being taken away.

The subtle opening drive was more justification for Belichick's and offensive coordinator Charlie Weis's support of Brady. No matter where he was, Brady never panicked. He had begun with his back to the goal and completed his "normal" slant to Brown. Five plays later, the Patriots hadn't scored, but they had won the field-position game: Brady was handed the ball at his own 3 and gave it up with St. Louis at its own 20.

That's the kind of quarterbacking they liked.

St. Louis had a 3–0 lead after one quarter, and that was okay with Belichick too. The game was slow and physical, and the Rams were earning their yards gradually. It took them ten plays to get their points—on a 50-yard Jeff Wilkins field goal—and that wasn't their style. They had another ten-play drive end in the second quarter when Wilkins missed a 52-yarder.

People in Missouri must have known then that there

was trouble. This was not the animated "Greatest Show" they had been used to watching. This was someone presenting the storyboards, one at a time. The Rams just didn't march for twenty plays to pull only 3 points out of their pockets.

Six minutes into the second quarter, things got worse. Crennel called for a play—"Turkey Zero"—that forced a smile out of Rob Ryan's father, who was sitting in the Superdome stands. Buddy Ryan was the founder of the "46," a pressure defense that leaves cornerbacks in man-to-man coverage with receivers. "Turkey Zero" is a "46" call, and the Rams weren't prepared for it on first down from their 39. Linebacker Mike Vrabel rushed from the left, expecting to find some resistance from Rams right tackle Rod Jones. There was none. Vrabel slammed into Warner, and Warner threw to where he thought Bruce would be.

Bruce was there. So was Patriots cornerback Ty Law, who was always telling people that defensive backs would embarrass receivers if they switched roles for a day. Indeed, he closed on the underthrown ball like a Pro Bowl corner and caught it like a Pro Bowl receiver at the Rams' 47. He was gone. There was the Patriots' sideline to his left, the end zone straight ahead, and gasps and flashing lights all around him. He cradled the ball in his left hand and raised his right arm to the domed sky.

"Now pat it down, big boy!" said his college buddy Steve King, who was watching the game with a group of Rams fans. Law "patted" it down, an end zone ritual that ended with him appearing to sweep up an invisible mess, from left to right.

Did the crowd know yet that this was going to be a game? Did the people at neutral Super Bowl parties around the country and world know? It may have happened because of a turnover, but the Patriots were able to do in one play what the Rams hadn't accomplished in 30. They scored a touchdown. And they weren't done.

For all of Martz's offensive innovations, he did have some weak spots. At times it seemed as if small things irritated him. He could be like the customer at the convenience store, paying for a newspaper with his Gold Card when dropping a couple of quarters would be more efficient. He found himself in that situation on the series following Warner's interception. On second-and-1 from the 50, Martz called for a Faulk run. Middle linebacker Tedy Bruschi stopped Faulk for no gain. But on third-and-1, Martz elected to go with a pass instead of a play for the exceptional Faulk, and the pass was incomplete.

Punt.

This allowed the Patriots to possess the ball for the next four and a half minutes. This was precisely their enthusiastic alternative to scoring. Their collaborative game plan was very good, but it was also time-sensitive. Belichick knew that the St. Louis offense wasn't likely to be quieted for an entire game. If the Patriots couldn't score, they weren't going to do anything stupid that would spark the Rams.

Just before the half, Belichick and Weis got a chance to experiment with a play they had changed in Friday's practice. Ricky Proehl fumbled after catching a 15-yard pass from Warner. There were eighty seconds left in the half, and Brady was taking over at the St. Louis 40. Four shotgun plays moved the Patriots to the Rams' 8 with thirty-six seconds left. They called timeout. Now they were revisiting the scenario from Friday.

"You know," Belichick said on Friday, "those goddamn corners are just sitting on the goal line. It's going to be hard to hit the out because they're just jumping it. These guys are right on the goal line. It's just going to be too tight."

So the play—"F Right 50 Quick Out Go Slant"— was changed from an out to an out and up. Receiver David Patten sold the double move perfectly, and Brady found him in the back of the end zone. The play was reviewed, just to be certain that Patten's feet were inbounds. They were. New England was ahead after two quarters, 14–3, and most people hadn't thought that was even possible.

It had truly become a waiting game in the third. Those who knew the Rams kept waiting for that burst. Waiting for Warner to drop back and dump a short pass to Faulk, waiting to watch Faulk make every right decision in traffic before getting into the clear for 25 or 30 yards. Those who watched this group of supposedly substandard Patriots kept waiting to see how long they could delay what the audience had become so accustomed to witnessing.

The Rams burned two of their three timeouts, threw one interception, and had no points in the third. The Patriots got a field goal from Vinatieri. It was 17–3 going into the final quarter, and something unlikely was going to happen. Either the Rams were going to counter the Patriots' concepts with some of their own and win this game late. Or the Patriots, winners of five games in 2000, were going to hold on for one of the greatest upsets ever seen in professional sports.

Finally, in the fourth, the Rams started to look familiar. Warner and the "Show" tunes were finding some rhythm: 14 yards to Az-Zahir Hakim, 9 yards to Ernie Conwell, 22 yards to Faulk. They had driven to the New England 9 with twelve minutes left. Belichick's team was exhausted. Warner chipped off 6 more yards with a pass to Jeff Robinson, and the Rams were 3 yards away from slicing the lead in half.

After Warner threw two incomplete passes, Martz made two bold calls. He wanted to go for a touchdown on fourth-and-goal from the 3. And he wanted a timeout to talk about the approach. There were ten and a half minutes remaining; he was spending his last available timeout.

Back on the field for the play, Warner had to improvise. When the week began, Belichick said he wanted to take away the quarterback's primary option and make him hold the ball. His primary option, Faulk, was covered. So he held. Then he began to scramble to his right. Only fate could concoct what Warner was facing now: he was being chased by linebacker Roman Phifer, a thirty-three-year-old veteran who began his career with the Rams—the *Los Angeles* Rams. Phifer pursued at such an angle that almost anything he did was going to be bad for Warner. He had cut off a passing lane and was in position to make the tackle.

"Now get his ass, Phife!" Ryan, his position coach, screamed from the coaches' box.

Phifer grabbed Warner and the ball was sprung from his hands. There it was, lying on the 3, there for safety Tebucky Jones to pick up and run with the other way. Upset? This was on its way to being a blowout. Jones ran down the field, and some of the Patriots on the sideline instinctively ran with him. Antwan Harris was one of those sideline players, and in the excitement he didn't notice that there was an eighty-three-year-old man standing behind him. It was Steve Belichick, who had been attending practices all week. The elder Belichick wound up on the ground as

Jones ran by with what appeared to be a 97-yard fumble return for a touchdown.

As Belichick was helped to his feet, he didn't want to talk about himself. He was asked if he was all right and he replied, "Hell, yeah. I'm fine." He was more concerned about the flag lying in the opposite end zone. "Sonofabitch," he sighed. Robert Kraft saw the flag as well. He briefly thought of Bill Buckner and the baseball championship that slipped through the legs of New England in 1986.

Faulk hadn't been open because Willie McGinest had him in a bear hug. It was an easy call to make. Holding, New England. Two plays later, Warner ran 2 yards up the middle for the first St. Louis touchdown of the day.

It had taken fifty minutes for the Rams to solve the Patriots' riddle. They were officially hackers now, having finally decoded the system. *We are playing our asses off,* Belichick thought. *But we're starting to wear down.* And that was just the defensive story. The Patriots weren't doing much on offense. Brady could recite all the variations of the Rams' "Cover 2" defense, but he couldn't find a way to get much movement against it. After the Warner touchdown, the Patriots answered with three plays and 8 yards. They held the ball for about a minute and a half before punting it away.

The game was turning. The Krafts, sitting in a seventh-level box, weren't interested in the news at their door: someone from the NFL wanted to escort them to the field to watch the final few minutes of the game. They didn't move. They were reminded again, and Robert Kraft made it simple. "If we win, they're not going to start the postgame without us. So we're going to wait to see what happens." The owner waited. There were casual fans in the box, and there was a professional—Saints coach Jim Haslett—in there too. Everyone knew the Rams were capable of tying the game late. There was also the chance that they'd win it.

The league's MVP now had the ball with seven minutes and forty-four seconds to play. The Patriots were winning, but Warner had leverage. He knew that their defense, which had just been on the field ninety seconds earlier, was in retreat. He started from his 7. Eighty seconds later he had the team at midfield. Plenty of time. Six minutes and seventeen seconds to play. He drove the team to the New England 38, but here were those conceptualists rising again. They had thrown off his timing just so, and he was holding the ball with no place to go. McGinest was approaching one second and on him the next. Sack. Second-and-9 had become third-and-25.

This time Belichick wanted the timeout. It was his last one. He saw how worn down his team was, and he obviously saw the stakes. He consulted with "RAC," which was what Crennel's colleagues called him.

"RAC, we can't give up this play. We can't give up a first down on third-and-25. I mean, that will kill us."

Having known Belichick since 1981, when both were Giants coaches, Crennel knew that "We can't give up this play" was a lot more layered and accusatory than it sounded. It really meant that there was no excuse for anyone—player or coordinator—to make a mistake at this moment in the game. It really meant that champions make these plays and that a bad, poorly coached defense is one that has no hope of getting off the field on third down.

Back on the field Warner attempted to pick up the first

by finding Holt near the sideline. The pass was incomplete. There were four minutes to play. If the Patriots could squeeze out a couple of first downs, this game was theirs. With no timeouts, the Rams weren't going to be able to stop the clock.

But there would be no firsts for the Patriots. They gave the ball to Antowain Smith, the running back who had done a good job all day. He lost 2 yards. Brady threw a safe pass to Smith on the next play—"0 Flood 130 D Pivot X In." It was a 4-yard gain to the Patriots' own 22. Thinking about the clock at this point, Weis told Brady to go with Smith again. They got 3 yards out of that run and were forced to punt.

Now the brilliance of the Rams shone: they got the ball at their 45 with 1 minute and 51 seconds to play. Twenty-one seconds later the game was tied. The Patriots were blitzing and in man-to-man coverage. Proehl got open, took an 11-yard pass from Warner, and ran 15 yards after the catch for a score.

Seventeen apiece, with 1:21 to play.

The Rams' sideline was energized, and the Superdome itself was pulsating with murmurs and anticipation. In the Fox TV booth, analyst John Madden was saying that the Patriots—at their own 17 with no timeouts—should play for overtime.

In the huddle Brady was unaware of any extraneous sound. He was never one to wander while he was working. He was at work now. He grew up loving sports and competition so much that he would ask his parents if he could wear his team uniforms to church. He went to the University of Michigan, where he wouldn't sleep on nights that he threw interceptions inside of two minutes—and those were two-minute drills in practice. If he hadn't been good at football, he would have become a businessman. Winning was his business these days, and he didn't want to be congratulated for thinking that way. Winning—and winning late—is what good quarterbacks are supposed to do.

So while the drama of the game may have excited many, he was calm when he heard Weis's voice in his helmet: "Okay, Tommy. 'Gun F Left 51 Go/OPEQ.' Look for Patten versus man. If not, Troy or J. R. Be careful with the ball."

He was careful. "J. R." was third-down back J. R. Redmond. He was Brady's man on the first two plays, good for 13 yards.

"Clock it, Tommy," Weis said.

He spiked the ball into the turf. There were forty-one seconds left, and his team was positioned at its 30. This was going to happen. *All I have to do is recognize the coverage, make sure guys are lined up right, read my progressions, and make the throw.*

"'Gun Trips RT 64 Under X Go.'"

He found Redmond again. This time it was an 11-yard gain, and Redmond stepped out of bounds to save time.

They were at their 41. They had thirty-three seconds left. They had the best kicker in the game simulating kicks on the sideline. This was going to be easy. He missed on "G Patriot RT 64 MAX ALL IN XQ"—for Brown—so the same play was called again.

Brown caught the ball over the middle, ran 23 yards, and stepped out of bounds at the Rams' 36. Brady knew Vinatieri could make it from here. But there was time to get him closer.

"'Gun Trips RT 68 Return.' Tommy, throw it to Wiggins and then clock it."

He located Jermaine Wiggins, the tight end from East Boston, for 6 yards. He clocked it with seven seconds remaining. The ball fell to the turf and then bounced up again into his waiting hands. He held it as if he were posing for a picture. Bringing style to the mundane, the sixth-round pick suddenly looked cool.

Vinatieri would step out soon to attempt a 48-yard field goal. Who wouldn't want a good kicker now? What coach wouldn't want his kicker to be his most consistent player in a situation like this? Perceptions and legacies were going to be affected with this attempt.

Patriots and patriots alike wanted this kick to be good. Just to say I told you so. Just to prove that substance and grit and unity were not outdated terms. Everyone could relate to not being tall enough, slim enough, fast enough, rich enough, young or old enough. That was the Patriots' appeal. Their roster and their staff were filled with people who were holding on to some previous slight that they couldn't or wouldn't forget.

Lots of people were on their feet now, holding hands or hoping for a miss. Veteran defensive end Anthony Pleasant was on the sideline, thinking of his friend Rob Burnett, who had won a ring the previous year with the Baltimore Ravens. Pleasant also thought of Scott Norwood. "Make it," he whispered. "I hope we don't do like Buffalo." Gil Santos was setting the scene for his listeners in New England. Santos, the radio voice of the Patriots, was concerned with the details first. Down, distance, placement. He liked to let people know the snapper (Lonie Paxton) and the holder (Ken Walter). "If it gets screwed up—if the snap is high or low—you want the people to have a sense of what happened," he once explained.

Vinatieri, man of routine, was walking toward the field. He was trying to concentrate, but he heard chatter from his own team. It was tight end Rod Rutledge, taunting one of the Rams.

"Yeah, motherfucker. We about to win the Bowl."

Walter knew Vinatieri wanted to say something, and he knew that this wasn't the time for the kicker to be talking. "I'll handle this," he told Vinatieri. "Hey, Rod. Can you shut up?"

There was no more talking. The ball was snapped, the hold was impeccable, and the kick gave Vinatieri exactly what he had been seeking on Saturday night: perfection. The kick was worthy of its own frame, powerful and high and unmistakable. It was a poll with immediate returns, a dramatic moment that eliminated all dramatic excess. There was no wait to see if it would sneak inside a post or barely clear one. It was a center cut. Santos had been trained to look at the officials before commenting on a field goal, so there was some hesitation in his call: "The kick is up and it is . . . good. It's good. . . ." He was informing, smiling, crying, and embracing—his wife and son were in the booth—at the same time.

The Krafts were still in their box, with a panoramic view at the 50. They had a family hug for this kick, and they had a family hug for themselves. They remembered how the Patriots were almost moved to St. Louis in 1993 and how their family bought the team in '94. They remembered the financial and public relations messes—from bankruptcy to bombast to Bill Parcells—that forever trailed the Patriots through most of the 1980s and the 1990s. They remembered 1971, when they were the Krafts of Graylynn Road in

Newton. Just a family of season-ticket holders who were hoping Jim Plunkett could help deliver a championship.

In the coaches' box, Scott Pioli had been standing on the stairs between the first and second levels. He had been standing for the entire game, hoping that the team he helped build could find a way to win. When the kick went through, Pioli fell down the stairs and into tight ends coach Jeff Davidson. The box, tense and serious most of the time, erupted. Pioli hugged Davidson, Brian Daboll, Berj Najarian, everybody. They all lost themselves for a moment until someone mentioned that they had to leave the box and head to the field.

There was red, white, and blue confetti on the carpet as the organization celebrated. Belichick, now finally and rightly clear of Parcells's shadow, was hugged by his daughter Amanda and lifted in the air by safety Lawyer Milloy. McGinest was in tears. A group of Patriots scouts, in seats twenty rows from the field, congratulated each other and fans they had just met. Guard Mike Compton fell to his knees as if he were worshiping. Another lineman, Joe Andruzzi, carried the American flag. His brother, Jimmy Andruzzi, was a New York City firefighter who had barely escaped the Twin Towers on September 11.

Patriots 20, Rams 17. Everyone with any connection to the team began to move toward a roped-off area reserved for the champions. And, really, that meant all of them.

An hour after the game, Pioli and his wife, Dallas, walked from the Dome to the Fairmont. They had already cried, sharing the moment with Pioli's parents and all his buddies from back home in Washingtonville, New York—Matt, Tom, Paul, and John the Worm. Three friends from college were there as well. Pioli then received a call from his friend Mark Shapiro. Pioli and Shapiro had met when they both worked in Cleveland. They had talked of their championship dreams for years. Now Pioli was the director of player personnel for the Patriots, and Shapiro was the general manager of the Cleveland Indians.

"Scooter," Shapiro said, calling Pioli by his nickname, "great job, man. I just got two words for you: collar stays, dude!"

Shapiro had watched Pioli interviewed on TV. The collars on Pioli's shirt were pointing in the air. He had raced from the box—but not before taking a Super Bowl banner as a souvenir—to be on the field. Shapiro knew he could tease Pioli for looking frazzled on the night that he became a champion. He knew how hard it was to help build a team that was both successful and dignified. They both laughed, and not just because Pioli didn't have plastic collar stays. He wasn't even sure what they were.

Now it was time for Pioli and everyone else to exhale and wait until tomorrow before thinking about the '02 season. He tried to go to the team party, but it turned out that the selfless, anonymous team he put together was a little too anonymous for his own good. He wasn't recognized at the door and was told he couldn't get into the VIP section. He and Dallas decided they would hang out instead with their friends from home. Brady got into the party, where he relaxed with rapper Snoop Dogg.

"Look at this," Snoop said, standing in the Imperial

Ballroom. "It's the MVP of rap here with the MVP of the Super Bowl."

Belichick was also at the Fairmont, in the hotel bar. He had wanted to stop in at Pat O'Brien's in the French Quarter, but security had advised against it. There were thousands of people outside. They had just watched or heard about one of the best Super Bowls ever played. Belichick would be mobbed out there. So he sat with his wife, Debby, and a half-dozen friends. He drank Hurricanes, laughed, and talked football until 4:30 Monday morning. He slept for ninety minutes and then got ready for the day-after press conference with Brady and NFL commissioner Paul Tagliabue.

By noon he was on Northwest flight 9965. The team was leaving New Orleans for Boston, where there would be a downtown parade the next day. Belichick sat near Pioli on the plane, and they compared their lists for the expansion draft. Their Lombardi Trophy wasn't even twenty-four hours old. But shortly after takeoff, they had already begun thinking about how they could win another one.

REVERSAL OF FORTUNE

The man at the front of the room hates giving this speech, although he has never lacked the confidence to give it. Anyone who knows him can tell you that. Bill Belichick hates to stand there, his entire team and coaching staff before him, and talk about the phenomenon of intelligent men—some of the same men who only nine months before had been champions of their sport—playing dumb football. Or, as he said after the 28–10 loss to the Green Bay Packers, "We have a lot of smart guys in this room, but on the football field we play like a bunch of fucking morons."

If you are one of the players flinching at the harshness of these words, you might as well begin packing. There is no way you are going to last as a New England Patriot. This is one of the reasons the Patriots' college scouts are asked by their bosses, "Can this player handle tough coaching?" What they really want to know, without the euphemism, is whether a prospect can deal with being "motherfucked" when things are not going well.

Most of the players in this auditorium could. They had to. This is a profession where political correctness never caught on. There is no liaison in Human Resources who monitors the way your supervisor talks to you. The players know their head coach can be profane, even when he is not angry. He has an extensive vocabulary—expletives not included—but he stores it like a precious sports car when he is here. He knows ambiguity doesn't work in the NFL. Some people may not like his brand of bluntness, but at least they understand it. That's what's important in this business where misunderstandings lead to losses and layoffs.

He has visions of how football teams should be built and how the games should be played. He is secure enough to allow these visions to be inspected, four or five times per year, for soft spots and holes. There is frequent self-scouting and self-analysis, his version of 3,000-mile check-ups to see if everything is running well. He prefers to have advisers and scouts with strong opinions, and at times he demands that those opinions be stated. As with his preparation for the Super Bowl, he will ask the football people closest to him—Scott Pioli and Ernie Adams—what they think, unafraid to hear ideas that are inconsistent with his own. He does the same thing with his assistants and other coaches he speaks with by phone. There are times when he talks strategy with his friend Nick Saban, the head coach of Louisiana State University. Saban will explain how he approached a play or situation at LSU, and Belichick will shake his head and say, "That makes a lot of sense. Why didn't I think of that?"

It's hard to find something that irritates him more than a lack of preparation and thought. When potential free agents arrive in Foxboro, one of the first things they're shown is the computer system. They are told that the video guys—Jimmy Dee, Fernando Neto, and Steve Scarnecchia—are on the second floor. They are reminded that they can better understand their responsibilities simply by walking up a flight of stairs or clicking a mouse. Jimmy Dee is used to cornerbacks asking for tapes on wide receivers and safeties asking for breakdowns on tight ends.

There are actually written tests—no multiple-choice here—in which players show their position coaches that they have grasped the key points of the week. Prior to the Green Bay game, the quarterbacks were given a six-page test with some of the following questions:

- From the "Under Tom" front, what is their favorite blitz?
- If the Packers play "1 Weak," on what down and distance can we expect to see it? How do the corners play this coverage?
- The huddle call is "1 T 34 Bob/T39 Boss." Identify the "Mike" linebacker and explain your procedure.
- When running "R32 Away A Flip" vs. "1 Weak" or "8 Sky," what should you expect to do with the football?

The final question—not including the "What year was Bryant Westbrook drafted?" bonus—was, "What will you do this week in order to lead your team to victory?" It may have been on the quarterbacks' test, but it was understood that the question was for everybody.

At this Monday meeting, October 14, it is apparent that watching the game tape has annoyed Belichick. He likes to see a correlation between what has been taught and practiced and what happens on the field. He hasn't seen enough of it. He didn't see it in San Diego when LaDainian Tomlinson ran for 217 yards, and he didn't see it the previous day in Foxboro, when Ahman Green ran for 136. The Patriots are 3–3, one of the most penalized teams in the league, and terrible at stopping the run. "You want to sum up the season in one play?" he says. "I'll tell you what it is: Tim Dwight coming from 15 yards behind Tomlinson, *outrunning* Tomlinson, knocking our ass out of the way down the sideline, and then Tomlinson goes in for a touchdown. That one play. He's playing at one speed, at one kind of effort, and we're playing at another one."

Belichick still is several weeks away from a healthy personnel disagreement with defensive backs coach Eric Mangini. He still is several weeks away from conceding—in a production meeting with CBS—that the constant references to and expectations from Super Bowl XXXVI have made this a stressful season for his team. Right now, though, he doesn't want to talk about the complex psyche of a defending champion.

"It's really embarrassing," he tells the team. "It really is. It's embarrassing. Can't hit the snap count. Can't line up on side. There are fucking holding penalties in the defensive passing game every week for key conversions. There are holding penalties on offense, giving the ball away like we don't give a shit about it. Just turn it over to 'em. Leave the ball lying on the field there for five seconds while they come from 30 yards away to recover it. It's just dumb football, fellas."

He stands in the front of the room. They sit in black, theater-style seats with cherry-wood desktops swinging from the sides. If this is their movie, he is their unsparing critic. If this is their classroom, he is their hawk of a teacher.

"I'll tell you one other thing too," he says. "I've read a couple of comments. Now, I don't spend a lot of time reading the paper. I really don't. But I do watch a little about what we say and what we think. I've seen a couple comments here, some of the players talking about we need to get our 'swagger' back. Our attitude back. . . ." They have been around him long enough to know that he is about to debunk a myth. You can hear it in his pronunciation of the word, the way he spits it out in the light so everyone can see how ridiculous it is.

"You know what? We didn't have a 'swagger' last year. If you fucking think about it, we didn't have a swagger. What we had was a sense of urgency, a sense of urgency about playing well, being smart, and capitalizing on every opportunity and situation that came our way. . . . It wasn't about a fucking swagger. You can take that swagger and shove it up your ass, okay?"

He is a versatile man, one who can easily navigate the disparate worlds of NPR and rated-R. He attended Phillips Academy, the same prep school as U.S. presidents, Pulitzer Prize winners, Academy Award winners, and the architect who designed Central Park. He attended Wesleyan University, the same college attended by federal judges, directors and writers of popular movies, governors, and a lyricist for the Grateful Dead. He could have wielded power in their worlds, but he always wanted this one. He always wanted to know football as well as his father the coach and to know teaching as well as his mother the language instructor.

He always wanted to be here, a football answer man at the front of the room. Coaches who have worked with him have acknowledged that much: he either has the answers or knows where to find them quickly. If you listen to what he has to say, if you play it the way he asks you to, you'll be in position to fulfill the prophecy. He doesn't see the game in four quarters. He sees it as a series of situations—could be four, could be twelve—where he tries to force the other coaches to declare what they are doing before he declares what he's doing. That's part of the plan all week, finding all areas where he can tilt the field so his team has some type of advantage. There is no debate that the other team has strengths. What he and his staff try to deduce is the source of the strength and whether there's any repetition, so to speak, that makes a team look stronger than it really is.

If he were interviewing somewhere, he would ace that old standard question, "What do you know about our company?" Oh, only everything. He tries to go to the root of teams, systems, and coordinators. He is looking for obvious trends as well as clever ones. All of that, along with swift recognition of what a team is attempting to do, could be the difference in the game. In his mind, "halftime adjustments" is one of the worst clichés of all. You're always adjusting, declaring, bluffing. Wait until halftime to do all that and you may be out of it already.

During the week he takes a private investigator's approach to Sunday's game. He is watching tapes, talking on the phone to anyone who may have a morsel of insight, meeting with Ernie, meeting with Scott, meeting with the coaches, meeting with head trainer Jim Whalen, and studying practices and practice tape. He finds time to get on the treadmill, talk with his wife and three children, and grab a Styrofoam bowl of something from the Gillette Stadium cafeteria. It almost doesn't matter what's in the bowl. Whatever it is usually has a lot of salt added to it.

No one questions how much time he puts into this. No one questions how much he sees and remembers. (Talk about a memory: once, in dreary Buffalo, he and Ernie actually tried to count the number of times they'd seen the sun in western New York.) And no one speaks on the rough days when he goes in front of a group of men and tells them what he saw and what he is seeing.

When he asks right tackle Kenyatta Jones how long he is going to continue to get his ass kicked on a play called "Toss 38 Bob," everyone knows he is really asking the team the same thing he is asking Jones. It's one of his best devices. He knows how to craft critiques in such a way that they go from being personal evaluations to collective ones, and suddenly everyone feels accountable.

"Do we have to see that again next week, and the week after that? When is it going to get fixed? When? When are we going to run 'Toss 38 Bob' at least for no gain? Forget about gaining yardage. When are we going to run it at least back to the fucking line of scrimmage?

"How long is that shit going to take? When are we ever going to see—well, we did see one last week by Givens—but when are we going to see a chip on kickoff coverage? When is that going to happen again? When are we going to chip on coverage, help our teammates out, and free someone up on one of those returns? Two weeks, three weeks, four weeks, I don't know. But the sooner we get that shit fixed, the sooner we start doing it right, the better things will be."

He doesn't leave it like that. He never does. The obscenities are never the last thing the Patriots hear in their meetings. The essence of Belichick is that he is a problem solver. Since he has already clearly identified the problems, he is now here to offer solutions. The solutions are easy to follow. He tells his players he needs to see more effort, more concentration, and more discipline when it comes to doing their jobs. It's easy. Do what he asks you to do and you'll always have a chance.

On a November afternoon in 2002, Pioli was sitting in his Gillette Stadium office. There were several times during the day when the entire room rattled, as if it were located next to a subway station. The unexpected eruptions—from vehicles passing in a nearby concourse—smothered the music coming from Pioli's CD player. He was listening to Dave Brubeck, with Miles Davis on standby. Pioli had been on the phone all day.

One of his first calls was with Lions president Matt Millen. They talked about cornerback Jimmy Hitchcock for a while. The Patriots had released him and the Lions had picked him up. But since Hitchcock failed his physical— "Was it the ACL thing, Matt? When he came out of college, he never had an ACL"—the Lions had let him go too. Pioli told Millen that he'd like to visit with him on Thanksgiving, when the Patriots would be in Detroit. "I know you have some insight and I'd love to hear your thoughts," Pioli said into the phone. "I'm sure there are some similar battles we're fighting."

The Patriots were 5–5, coming off a 27–20 loss at Oakland. Ten games into the season, their deficiencies were apparent to casual fans and experts alike. They were old. They were slow. They couldn't stop the run. And they couldn't help referencing the year before. Pioli was on the phone so much because he was trying to do something to make it better. He had college tapes to view and draft reports to read, yes. But he also had to do something about right now.

He was trying to work out a deal with agent Brian Levy, who represented a linebacker named Jashon Sykes. Sykes was on the Broncos' practice squad, which technically made him a free agent. Sykes was twenty-three, stood six feet two inches, and weighed 236 pounds. Pioli thought he could help the Patriots that year and next. He planned to tell Levy that when they talked again, but here was another phone call getting in the way.

"Let me see what this is all about," he said. "This is Scott."

"Hey, Scott, this is Jason. How you doing?"

"Good. Thanks, Jason."

"Sorry to bother you. Just wanted to bring to your attention. I didn't know if you guys were looking for a kickoff specialist or not. But I have a kid—"

"Jason, are you working with someone?"

"Yeah, sorry about that. I didn't make that clear to your girl. But J. R. Jenkins—"

"No interest. We've got a full roster. I'm not sure—"

"But kickoff specialists are so hard to find. I guess Baltimore used him for that purpose—"

Pioli rolled his eyes. He brought out his sarcastic wit.

"I guess he can take Deion's job, huh?" he said, referring to impressive rookie Deion Branch.

"Yeah? Paying the same money?"

"I'm sure Deion would love that. People are calling to send us someone to take his job."

"Hey, I'm just looking out for my guy."

Pioli hung up.

"I get a hundred calls like that a week. The best is when you're losing games and they call you and tell you, 'Yeah, you guys are really struggling. It looks like you need some help on your offensive line.' I mean, how would you react to that? It's so insulting."

Jason insulted Pioli in many ways, and not just with his football comments. Pioli said he couldn't do his job without Nancy Meier, who has lived Patriots history since she was nineteen. She is a wife, a mother of two children, and a woman who has seen a whole lot of football.

"She's probably been in the league longer than he's been alive, and he's saying 'your girl.' He was pooping his diapers when she was fricking working in the league."

This was yet another sign that the Patriots were not the same team they were in 2001. When you are winning, these phone calls do not come. When your flaws are not obvious, you don't have Jasons on the periphery, tugging at your coat and telling you to look over here. The calls were reminders that the night in New Orleans, with the colors falling from the top of the Superdome, was from another football time zone. By any measure, 5–5 equals average. On an average day, average teams receive average phone calls.

"And when we get someone hurt, it's like pit bulls on pork chop underwear the day after a game. Somebody gets hurt, especially on a national game, my phone's ringing off the wall. A lot of it is ambulance chasing. I understand."

Meier told Pioli that the last flight from Denver to Boston was at 6:20. Theoretically, if Jashon Sykes decided to accept the $9,000 weekly raise that the Patriots were going to offer him, he could throw a few things in a travel bag and hop that 6:20. Sean Gustus, a recent Richmond University graduate who was trying to break into scouting, would pick him up at the airport. Gustus would drop him off at the Residence Inn and then return in the morning. There would be doctors to see, papers to sign, and new coaches and teammates to meet.

At least that was the plan. When Pioli talked with Sykes, there wasn't any noticeable excitement in the linebacker's voice. He attended Colorado University, and the feeling was that if the Broncos put him on their fifty-three-man roster, he would be content to stay in Denver. He didn't say that, although you could hear it.

"Why don't you give Brian a call back and then tell him to give me a call when you decide what you want to do," Pioli said to Sykes. "There's a six-twenty flight tonight out of Denver. It's the last flight getting you into Boston. And we could have you on the practice field tomorrow."

"Okay," Sykes said.

"All right, so give Brian a holler and give me a call."

"I will."

He didn't. Sykes was staying in Denver.

There are phone calls, draft meetings, contract negotiations, and film studies all folded into Pioli's job. But what it can be reduced to is this: every day he goes to the office wondering how and where he can find the right kind of players for Bill Belichick and the New England Patriots.

REVERSAL OF FORTUNE

■ ■ ■

There is nothing outwardly unusual about the Four Points Sheraton Hotel in Norwood, Massachusetts. It has a "casual upscale" restaurant on the first level, with sports showing on the televisions near the bar. It has a spacious ballroom, which has been the site of numerous class reunions and wedding receptions. On the second floor, at the top of the stairs and to the right, it has a conference room that resembles hundreds of others in the state. But the conference room becomes distinct, at least on several Saturday nights in the fall and early winter. The room becomes the place where 20 men meet and review the plan for the Patriots' game the next day.

Many of these men, the members of Bill Belichick's football Cabinet, could sit among the sports fans at the bar and remain unnoticed for hours. They are assistant coaches, coaching assistants, and members of the support staff. They are officially silent, permitted to speak with the media only on special occasions, yet each of them has control over an aspect of the game and is equally responsible for helping to shape and enforce Patriots policy. Their biggest fear is a team breakdown in general and a breakdown in their department in particular. They work for an organization where accountability is one of the sacred codes: there is no place to hide if things get sloppy. And if sloppiness happens too often, they know that the sympathy card cliché—"We all have bad days at the office; we'll get 'em tomorrow"— will not console the bosses.

Romeo Crennel is in charge of the department in which Belichick made his name. Defense. He explains the simple coaching ethos: "When we lose, I always feel like there's something I did wrong. There's something I could have done better—there's a call I should have made to help us. I think if you're going to survive in this business, you cannot accept losing, you don't like losing, and you take losses extremely hard. I take losses hard because I have to: if you lose, you're going to get fired."

The coaches—different ages, races, and politics—are as diverse as the routes they took to the NFL.

One of them, Jeff Davidson, was the starting left tackle who protected John Elway's blind side in 1991. The Denver Broncos drafted Davidson in the fifth round in 1990, two rounds before they selected a receiver out of Savannah State named Shannon Sharpe. Another assistant, Rob Ryan, was the only white coach on an all-black staff at a historically black university in Nashville. Ryan used to gas up a 1989 Thunderbird and travel through Georgia and Florida trying to convince young men that there were many academic and athletic reasons to choose a school such as Tennessee State. "And then I'd remind them that the school's female-to-male ratio was seventeen to one," he says. One coach, Eric Mangini, is a member of Chi Psi, which makes him Belichick's fraternity brother. That status didn't get him any special privileges in Cleveland, where he handed out media notes in the press box and picked up dirty jerseys in the locker room. One worker, Brian Smith, is an avid hip-hop fan and 2004 Providence College honors graduate. He was nicknamed "Reeses" by receivers coach Brian Daboll because "he's not cool enough to be Eminem."

Biology does not make all of them a family; time and aspirations do. When they arrived in Norwood on December 7,

2002, it was the 145th day of their football season. With an exception or two, they had spent all of those days—Thanksgiving included—together. Whether it was at the hotel for seven A.M. coaches' meetings or at Gillette Stadium for staff meetings in the afternoon, they were always discussing ways to win football games. A few of them are quietly talented strategists themselves, destined to one day lead their own "programs." Followers of pro teams usually don't call them programs, but that's exactly what Belichick is trying to build in New England. He wants coaches and scouts to be developed in the Patriots system, just as players are.

It's part of the reason football operations will always have a few young and smart trainees, thirty-and-under football enthusiasts who can come into the company at entry level and be promoted in two or three seasons. Daboll and Josh McDaniels arrived in Foxboro as coaching assistants. Both became position coaches before turning thirty. As a teenager, Smith performed several odd jobs with the Patriots and still found time to excel in his classes. Now he is the team's director of operations. Nick Caserio was hired as a personnel assistant in 2001 and became an area scout in 2003. They join veterans such as Charlie Weis, Mike Woicik, and Dante Scarnecchia, father of video assistant Steve Scarnecchia. All of them understand what's expected of them, from the team meetings in Foxboro on Monday afternoons to the coaches' meetings in Norwood on Saturday nights.

"All he wants is perfection," says Ryan, who is now the defensive coordinator of the Oakland Raiders. "If you can give him perfection, you'll be all right. He wants it as close as you can get. And he knows what you have to give."

Some of the coaches are less tolerant of their own imperfections than Belichick himself. Once during training camp there was a scheduling miscommunication that led to strength-and-conditioning coach Woicik arriving late for a practice. Belichick understood that it wasn't Woicick's fault, but the strength coach was torn up about it. He showed up at Belichick's office and tried to pay a fine. But the coach, knowing Woicik's thoroughness, wouldn't accept it.

On Saturdays, sometimes the coaches arrive in the conference room before Belichick does. The conversation is often light and humorous, with the coaches teasing each other about their picks in the office college football pool or a loss by someone's alma mater. When Belichick approaches and walks toward the head of the long conference table, it's as if the judge has entered the courtroom. He rarely jokes in these meetings. Most of the humor comes from comments he makes in the context of player or game evaluation. He is not easily pleased, and neither are they. He goes around the room and gets final status reports from Crennel, Weis, Woicik, and special-teams coach Brad Seely. He misses nothing—weather, officials, inactives, what's at stake.

At the December 7 meeting, the Patriots were 7–5 and seeking their fifth win in six weeks. They would play Drew Bledsoe and the Buffalo Bills—for the second time that season—the next day at Gillette. After a four-game losing streak, the Patriots were now beginning to climb toward the top of the AFC East standings. They had ended their skid a month earlier in Buffalo, winning 38–7. A few days before the November 3 Buffalo game, Belichick sensed two issues that could cause the slide to continue: selfishness and too much focus on Bledsoe. He touched on both in an

October 28 team meeting, leaving no doubts about his position on both subjects.

"We need to have everybody together on this team. Now, there's not one person in this room—not one—who can't improve. And it starts with me. I'll sit down with any of you and show you where you can improve. Any of you. Okay? So all of us can be better and need to be better. That's where your focus needs to be: what can you do better to help this football team? There's not going to be any toleration for 'I'm doing my job, someone else can do theirs better.' Well, maybe they can. But all of us need to do a better fuckin' job too. So let's start with that and move forward."

This season was frustrating him, on the field and in the meetings. He questioned himself several times, wondering if he and his staff had properly prepared the players. Were they giving them things that they couldn't handle? Were they making themselves clear? After the team's fourth consecutive loss, 24–16 against Denver, a dejected Belichick had retreated to his office and had a long conversation with Scott Pioli. The team had warts, sure, and some of them couldn't be corrected until the off-season. But other things—attitude and communication—could be fixed before training camp of 2003. He wanted to make that clear in the October meeting.

"You've got three choices," he continued. "Talk about yourself, either say something constructive or be supportive. Otherwise, shut the fuck up. Okay? Shut the fuck up. We don't need anything other than one of those three options. Either you get better, you support someone else who is trying to get better, or you have a constructive suggestion that will help this football team. If it will help, we'd all love to hear it. Otherwise, shut the fuck up, all right? And let's look in a positive direction. Everybody understand that? That's the only way it's going to work, fellas. Stick together as a team, support each other as a team."

He knew his trade of Bledsoe would be reprised and analyzed all week. He knew that there were still pockets of Bledsoe supporters, inside the organization and out.

"Obviously there's going to be some extracurricular activity this week as far as press and the media and TV and everybody else talking about a lot of other shit besides the game itself. Let's cut right to the chase: I'm responsible for making personnel decisions on this team. I made them two years ago, I made them last year, I make them this year, and I'll make them next year. So if there's any personnel decision made on this team, ultimately I'm the one who is going to be responsible for it. You guys aren't making them. You guys really don't have any input into making them. So just refer everything to me and stay out of it. . . . Don't worry about last year or last week or the off-season. Don't worry about any of that shit. If I have to answer it, I'll answer it. You guys don't have to worry about that. It wasn't your decision, it's not your job, and it's really not anything that you need to concentrate on."

They went to Buffalo later in the week and began Sunday afternoon by scoring the game's first 17 points. They led 31–7 after three quarters and were never threatened. As one of the team buses cruised away from the stadium and toward the airport, Mangini looked out the window and saw debris strewn in the parking lots and the last fires simmering from tailgaters' grills. "It looks like one of those scenes from the end of a war," he said.

REVERSAL OF FORTUNE

■　■　■

Back in the Sheraton a month later, it is time to approach Buffalo again. If New England can win the game, it will make the Patriots' record against the Bills 5–1 since 2000.

"Until they have some success against us, there's got to be some doubt," Belichick says to the coaches. "They don't know if they can beat us."

He asks Woicik about defensive lineman Rick Lyle, and Woicik says he plans to work him out before the game. He asks about the health of safety Tebucky Jones, and he is assured that Jones will be ready to play. He goes over the list of possible inactives, and he asks Weis if he has a strong opinion on either going into the game with an eighth lineman or going with seven and making tight end Cam Cleeland active. "I'm indifferent," Weis says. He decides to activate Cleeland and leave Greg Randall, Tom Ashworth, and Russ Hochstein inactive. He says the team had a good week of practice, and he wants to see if Buffalo can sustain an eight- to ten-play drive.

No one is animated during these rundowns, no matter how strong the statements are. The coaches are dressed casually, but the room has the spirit of a business meeting. There have been elements of game-plan review during the week, but this is the only time when it all comes together for everyone to see and hear. This is the time to remind everyone that the Patriots must throw on the Buffalo safeties and break tackles in the secondary. There is a note to "throw deep or deeper routes on Clements (not 10- to 12-yard routes unless pressed)." Clements is cornerback Nate Clements, whom the offensive coaches believe to be vulnerable deep. They have also noticed that the Buffalo safeties bite hard on play-action passes.

They are comfortable with the way they plan to defend Bledsoe. And they have a grasp of what the Bills are going to attempt against them. Buffalo's primary defensive coverage is "Cover 8." The Bills' safeties line up 9 to 12 yards deep and rotate on the snap. They make it difficult for teams to detect any pre-snap rotation. The weak safety and weak corner line up even and then rotate on the snap. It is mentioned that last year Buffalo's approach played as "Cover 8 Weak Sky." There are six single-spaced pages of notes on the Bills. It is up to the Cabinet to reduce its detailed information into digestible points that players can remember when they are on the field trying to control Bledsoe and jam Peerless Price and Eric Moulds. Each coach brings his own twist and own experience to getting the message across. The beauty and measure of temporary relief comes on Sunday evenings, when the message has been received and the game has been won.

Winning Sundays are the most quiet and satisfying moments of the week. They are quiet because, for those wearing headsets, the loud voice traffic in their heads is gone. They don't realize how much noise is there until they remove the headsets and no longer feel the rush of competition, intensified by the desires of 70,000 fans. During the game the coordinators are receiving information from the coaches in the box: down and distance, formation, their sense of what the other team is going to attempt to do. The coordinators then take that information and make a quick decision on what the call will be, relaying it either to quarterback Tom Brady, if you're Weis, or to the defensive players on the field, if you're Crennel.

"It's the competition," Crennel says. "It's the crowd—although you try to tune the crowd out. It's the challenge and excitement of 'Okay, it's third-and-8. What is this guy going to call? What am I going to call? Can I make the play? Can my guys make the play and get off the field? And can we do it enough to win the game?'" Sometimes Belichick's deep voice can be heard over the headsets: "Good call." He watches the game and makes decisions when his authority is needed. If he sees something developing, he'll tell his coordinators so it can be reflected in their calls. His mission is always to subtly lift the field, like a man lifting a car hood, so opponents will be slightly off balance and never quite right as they try to sustain drives. He is so relentless with study and preparation because of game day. What good is it if he sees it and no one else does? He wants them all to see it. He would actually prefer that his players make their own adjustments on the sideline instead of watching the game.

Pioli does watch the game. He is upstairs in the coaching box, a box too small to contain the competitive zeal of men who define their professional success by what happens on the field. For them, there are no throwaway plays. Every call on both sides of the ball was carefully selected, their response to something they see or anticipate seeing from the other team. There is never a moment of impulse: no one ever shouts into the headsets, "Hell, let's just throw it deep." A few times during the game a team will come out in a formation that is not part of its usual package. "I smell shit, RAC," Ryan will warn. "Look out for a trick here."

Often, Belichick will be buzzed during the game. It will be Ernie Adams, who is intensely watching—with headsets—from the coaches' box. "Bill, I'm expecting some kind of pressure here," Adams will say. Or he'll review a controversial call and handicap the coach's chances of success on a challenge. "A catch is defined as firm grasp and control, and he doesn't have it," Adams will report. "Let's challenge this one."

The manic NFL coaching atmosphere tends to attract smart risk-takers who love the mixture of physical and intellectual competition. It is like that in New England and in other cities throughout the league. The average NFL team is a storefront propped before the public, with a range of activity going on in backrooms. Assistants and staff members who will not be featured in media reports lead these activities, which are sometimes as basic as listening to venting or making runs to the airport. What makes the leaders of Patriots football operations different from heads of some companies is the value they place on jobs that have no glamour. They truly respect those who do grunt work, so much so that they are willing to promote them if they show the aptitude to be promoted.

Belichick is trying to construct a meritocracy where no one is placed in a categorical box and chained there for the rest of his coaching career. He looks at his own start in coaching, with little pay and not even a piece of glory in black and white. (In the official Colts history, he is not listed on the coaches' page.) If others are willing to take a similar path, without whining about it, he knows he has someone special. That's why he has so much confidence during his coaches' meetings and during games: hard workers surround him.

In Woicik he knows he has someone who takes all assignments seriously. Before each game officials ask Belichick who his "get-back coach" is. It is Woicik. The get-back coach is the one who makes sure players are not too close to the sideline. The first time Belichick gave Woicik the job, Woicik was so into it that Belichick said he had never seen anyone do it better. The strength coach also impressed him when he arrived for his job interview with detailed charts and presentations. Woicik has a thick booklet for the Patriots' off-season program. It includes everything from his pyramid of physical success—skill, movement, power, strength, conditioning, flexibility—to his attention to nutrition and recovery. Players reading Woicik's manual never lack information. He even includes grocery lists and fat analyses of food from fast-food chains McDonald's, Burger King, Dairy Queen, KFC, and Taco Bell.

In Crennel, Belichick sees a man who chased football in Kentucky, Texas, Georgia, and Mississippi. He was at Ole Miss just sixteen years after James Meredith became the first black student to integrate the Oxford campus. Crennel, who is black, talked with his wife before taking the Ole Miss job. She said she'd be willing to give it a try.

"Probably the biggest thing that made you wonder was the Rebel flag and the Klan and all that," he says. "But if you were helping their team to win, even though they might have some of those vices in the back of their minds, they'd choose to forget about it for a little while. My experience in Mississippi was not a bad one, because the people I dealt with wanted to be helpful." Crennel went from Ole Miss to Georgia Tech, and from Georgia Tech to the New York Giants.

While in New York, Crennel, Belichick, and Weis all worked together. Weis was a Giants coaching assistant in 1990, nine years after Crennel began there. He had been a head coach in high school and an assistant coach in college before going to New York. Weis remembers a conversation he had with Belichick in '90, the week before a November 18 game with the Lions. Detroit was on its way to scoring the fifth-most points in the NFL, and Weis told Belichick he had some ideas about the team's run-and-shoot offense. "Let's hear them," Belichick said. Weis told him what he knew. The Giants won the game 20–0, limiting the Lions to 208 total yards. Weis says he never forgot how gracious it was of Belichick to mention him—an assistant to the assistants—when speaking with the media afterward.

Brady says Weis's creativity and toughness inspire him. "Charlie goes through surgery where he almost died, and he's back trying to coach us," Brady marvels. The coach had gastric bypass surgery in the summer of 2002. He thought the procedure was going to be an uncomplicated one, but he came so close to death, owing to excessive internal bleeding, that he was twice given last rites. He remembers waking up in the hospital and seeing Brady in his room.

It was Brady who also said that he enjoyed playing football because it was an opportunity for him to be around like-minded "high achievers" who love the game. It's the same with the coaching staff. Some of them, like Davidson, Pepper Johnson, and Markus Paul, played in the NFL. Others, such as Belichick, Weis, and Ivan Fears, did not. The link is that they are high achievers, immersed in a scrupulous culture of winning.

On December 8, a windy Sunday in Foxboro, the Patriots prepared for Bledsoe's return to New England. The quarterback was a well-liked player in the region, and he gained new fans on his way to Buffalo. Before leaving, he placed full-page ads in both the *Boston Globe* and the *Boston Herald,* thanking local fans for their support. The fact that he was traded was not a surprise; the fact that he went to Buffalo was startling.

The Patriots were willing to risk trading a former Pro Bowl player to a team in their own division. They were willing to trade him to a team with an offensive coordinator, Kevin Gilbride, who enjoyed long passes as much as Bledsoe did. The Bills had Moulds and Price, two receivers on their way to 1,200-yard seasons. It appeared to be a good match. The Bills had a record of 6–6, trailing the Patriots by one game in the division. They had beaten Miami the previous week, 38–21.

Mangini, the Patriots defensive backs coach, was ready for the return. Before the game in Buffalo, he had given his players a sheet outlining the Bills' passing principles. Some of the same rules applied a month later:

- This offense is built on vertical routes and big plays. The coordinator is pass-oriented, and Drew wants to throw the ball down the field.
- We must force Drew to throw into tight coverage or hold the football. Do not give up any easy completions.
- There will be some game-plan formations, but they will be limited. They have not run any bunch or stacked receivers this season.
- The Bills will run their two-minute offense anywhere on the field.
- There has been no shifting and very little motion. What you see is pretty much what it will be.

As the coaches had discussed the night before, Woicik had indeed worked out Jones and declared him ready to play. So that would help Mangini's unit as well. Victor Green would start, but Jones would be able to contribute. He would soon be in position to make one of the best plays of the game.

When it was time to play, Bledsoe stepped on the field to a nice ovation. It was respectful and a bit restrained, a collective tip of the cap but nothing too indulgent. It was the nicest thing that would happen to him all day. He and his teammates couldn't get into a flow at all. They appeared to have a 27-yard completion to the New England 15, but an illegal motion penalty wiped it out and they were forced to punt. They were still in the game in the first quarter, even though they were down 10–0, when Bledsoe threw a pass that was intercepted by lineman Richard Seymour. Two plays later, Brady threw a 9-yard touchdown pass to receiver Donald Hayes.

Seventeen to nothing. Now Bledsoe was really playing into the Patriots' hands, because he was going to have to do what they expected anyway: throw it long. They were ready for him. He was able to prove Belichick wrong in one sense. He was able to end the first quarter and begin the second with a long drive, a drive that exceeded eight to ten plays. He was able to lead a fourteen-play drive from his own 9 all the way to the New England 1. But on second down, he dropped back to pass and tried to force the ball into coverage. Jones was watching him the whole time, anticipating the throw. The ball was thrown for tight end Dave Moore, but it was a poor throw and a poor decision. Jones intercepted it. The Patriots converted the turnover into 3 points, and now it was a matter of running out the clock.

REVERSAL OF FORTUNE

The Bills weren't going to come back from a 20–0 deficit, although they did cut the lead in half in the third quarter. Once again, there were too many Buffalo mistakes. Price fumbled, and that led to an Antowain Smith touchdown run. And when Bledsoe touched the ball after that, he threw another interception, this one to Ty Law. He ended the day with four interceptions. The members of the Cabinet ended the day with hugs for each other and a few relaxing moments spent at home with their "other" families.

The Patriots were 8–5. They weren't winning games impressively, but everyone had a similar thought: they hadn't always been impressive the year before, and they won their last six regular-season games and captured the Super Bowl. As much as they had struggled in 2002, they didn't see any good reason why they couldn't go on a run of their own again. The reasons may not have been seen, but the reasons were there. In three weeks everyone would be forced to acknowledge that the season's best wasn't good enough. Why wasn't it good enough? That was something they'd have to argue about in their meetings.

WAIT TILL LAST YEAR

The driver was early. He was told to be at the main entrance of the Sheraton Music City Hotel at 8:15 on Sunday night, and he was there at 8:00 idling in his black sedan. He was just following instructions. He didn't know that the hundred-mile trip he was about to take would hold so much significance for the head coach of the New England Patriots. He didn't know that this trip from Nashville to Monterey would jog a lifetime of Bill Belichick's memories and, eventually, sadden his heart.

It was December 15, 2002, about twenty-four hours before the Patriots would play the Tennessee Titans on *Monday Night Football*. Belichick's day, which began in Foxboro, had already been full. He had overseen a Gillette Stadium practice at 10:45 that morning. There was a flight out of Providence at 1:30, an arrival at the hotel three hours later, a production meeting with ABC's John Madden, Al Michaels, and Melissa Stark, and finally a meeting with the coaching staff.

Now he was sitting in the backseat of a car, being driven eastbound on I-40 toward a small town near the foothills of the Cumberland Mountains. He was on his way to see his cousin, Jean Freeman. He had a feeling that it would be the last time he saw her alive. Jean had terminal cancer that had attacked her pancreas. Jean and Bill had spent a lot of time together, especially during holidays with his mother's family in Florida. They had always gotten along, talking about everything from school to music. She followed his career when he got into coaching, encouraged him, and bragged about him.

"Since I was an only child, she was as close to a sibling as anyone," he says.

He was going to make the trip as normal as possible. Christmas was ten days away, so he had a bag full of gifts for her in the trunk. After ninety minutes of driving, he was at her house, just off the highway. It was one of her good days, so she ran out of the house and met him at the car. She was a small woman, about a size 2, with a quick smile. She told him to come inside the modest house, and as he petted a brown dog named Bear she insisted on getting him a cup of coffee. Her aunt was in the living room, knitting and watching the Cardinals and Rams play the late NFL game on ESPN. She pulled Belichick close to her and whispered, "I'm so glad you came. This is good for Jean. You don't know how good this is for her." She smiled as her eyes filled with tears.

"So what's going on?" Jean shouted from the kitchen. "How are you?"

She told her famous cousin that she had been rooting for his Patriots to recapture what they had the previous season. She mentioned an interview she had seen with him on one of the networks. After she returned and handed him his coffee, she sat on the floor with her legs folded. She opened one of his gifts. Inside the box was a stylish shirt, a matching belt, and a bracelet. She was excited about the gifts and teased him: "Tell Debby I said thanks for picking these out." Belichick smiled.

They had a lot of fun that night. They caught up on family news. They played with Bear. They halfway watched the game, although Belichick did pay close attention when a promo for *SportsCenter* used a cheap tease and mentioned that the Red Sox had acquired Giambi. "What?" the coach said. "That can't be right." It was. The Red Sox had acquired the marginal Jeremy Giambi, not Jason, his All-Star brother. At one point the cousins got into a discussion that could have continued for hours. They were talking about some of their favorite music and favorite concerts. They went on and on about the Rolling Stones, Bon Jovi, Bruce Springsteen, Santana, and a group that Jean remembered seeing open for the Stones on their "Steel Wheels Tour." "Living Colour," she said. "Those guys were a lot of fun."

As they reminisced and laughed, she had a sudden thought. The driver—what had he been doing all this time? "You should have told him to come in," Jean said. "I feel bad that he's out there all by himself."

She knew that Belichick didn't want to leave, but she could also tell that he was tired. It was sneaking toward midnight, and he had a game the next night. She told him that he should probably head back to Nashville. Her aunt, who had sat in the living room the entire time they were there, knitting and smiling, told Belichick again how happy she was to see him. Jean walked her cousin to the car, gave him a hug, and told him she would talk with him later.

He really was tired. She had known him long enough to notice his fatigue before he did. She lived near a gas station, a Burger King, and a convenience store. Belichick asked the driver to stop at the store so he could pick up a Coke. He was trying to hold off sleep for twenty-five to thirty more minutes. Soon he would leave the little town with the beautiful scenery and affordable real estate.

He had been born in Tennessee fifty years earlier, way back when his father was coaching at Vanderbilt. This return to the region, with towns called Sparta and Algood and Pleasant Hill, was primarily a business trip. He had told Michaels, Madden, and Stark earlier that night that he was looking forward to seeing the Patriots play a good team on the road. "It will let us see where we're at," he said.

But it was a family trip as well. His visit to Monterey was uplifting in a way because he had seen Jean smiling and enjoying herself. But her condition would worsen six weeks later. She wasn't going to make it and he knew it. She died in January 2003.

He was going to remember this visit to Tennessee. Professionally, it was going to be humbling. There were going to be things in the Titans game that were going to make him question entire segments of his team. Personally, the trip was going to cause him to reflect. He was going to remember how friendly and extroverted his cousin had been the last time he saw her, even though she was in pain and not expected to survive until the spring. He was going to remember how quickly life changes. As a coach and as a cousin, he sometimes found himself looking back to the joy of last year.

The 2002 season was so good, early, that Tom Brady had to tell one of his teammates about it. Before the fourth game, at San Diego, Brady was standing next to receiver David Patten. The quarterback called Patten by his nickname.

"Chief," Brady said, "I was just thinking: we might go undefeated this year."

It felt that way in the beginning. In the first game against the Steelers, the Patriots were helped by new additions Deion Branch, Donald Hayes, Christian Fauria, and Victor Green. It was their first regular-season game in dazzling Gillette, their new stadium, completed in May 2002, and they won, 30–14. Branch's third-quarter block on Pittsburgh safety Lee Flowers was so impressive that it was a high-priority headset topic in the coaches' box. "Make sure you go over and congratulate his ass," assistant coach Jeff Davidson said to Charlie Weis. "He made a great block on that play."

The play was a touchdown pass from Brady to receiver Hayes, whom the Patriots had signed as a free agent from Carolina. At six feet four inches, Hayes was the Patriots' tallest receiver. The idea was that he would be able to use his height on routes that couldn't be thrown to the team's other wide-outs, all six feet and under. But there weren't many games that Hayes was comfortable with the offense, and there was a good reason for it. He hinted at it in October in an interview with Nick Cafardo of the *Boston Globe*.

Going into the 2000 draft, the Patriots had narrowed their choice of quarterbacks to two: Tom Brady of the University of Michigan and Tim Rattay of the University of Louisiana–Lafayette. They apparently picked the right one.

For half of the 2001 season, the weekly quarterbacks meetings were a drama of their own: the surprising Brady had taken the starting job, Bledsoe was the reluctant backup, and Belichick was their position coach. "There was discomfort in the room," Belichick said.

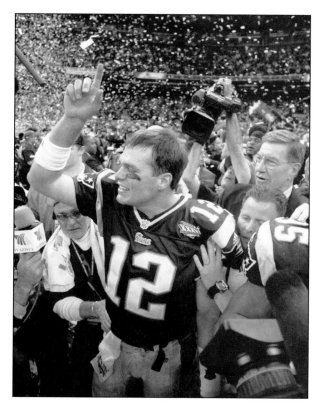

One of the biggest upsets in professional sports began to unfold with this Ty Law interception against the Rams.

Bob Kraft became a Patriots season-ticket holder in his late twenties—Myra didn't approve at the time—and spent most of his forties and early fifties trying to buy the team.

Adam Vinatieri's amazing work on the field and in the weight room earned him the distinction of being a football player—who just happened to be a kicker.

A quick-witted Vrabel, father or son, can usually get a laugh out of Belichick.

Rodney Harrison gave the 2003 secondary the production and toughness it lacked in 2002. He helped establish a fine system and made sure his teammates were conscious of rest and nutrition by frequently asking, "Are you hydrating?"

Having the thoughtful Brady, says Oakland Raiders defensive coordinator Rob Ryan, is like having Belichick on the field "with a better arm."

It wasn't so long ago that Brady couldn't get the attention of a young woman he liked at the University of Michigan. Now the bachelor, here with actress Bridget Moynahan, is rarely unnoticed, locally or nationally.

In November 2003, the Patriots used intellect and determination to prevent Peyton Manning and the Colts from gaining 1 yard in four tries. In January 2004, the Patriots were even tougher. Manning threw five interceptions in the AFC Championship game.

Scott Pioli and his friend Cleveland Indians general manager Mark Shapiro often spoke of building dignified championship teams. Shapiro reminded him of that after Super Bowl XXXVI—and also gave him a quick fashion tip.

No one has to balance the complexities of Belichick-Parcells more than Pioli. Belichick is his boss and one of his best friends. Parcells is his father-in-law.

Belichick says that Parcells's focus before Super Bowl XXXI was "totally inappropriate." Parcells left the Patriots for the Jets and took Belichick with him. Three seasons later, the longtime colleagues had a public split.

The passionate Lawyer Milloy was popular in New England because of his style of play. But when he was released in September 2003, the move triggered some commentary that Belichick would never forget.

At Andover, Belichick was a center and Ernie Adams (number 81) was a guard. They haven't been far from each other since. Belichick relies on Adams in the same way a president relies on a top adviser.

"My role right now is to get this offense down. I'm still not really there. Some days and some weeks I get it, and then on Sunday it's something totally different. . . . I don't want to be out there hurting the team. I'd rather sit on the sideline until I feel comfortable and I know the offense and the coaches know I know the offense."

What Hayes didn't say was what the Patriots already knew. He had a learning disability, and the multiple options in the New England passing game sometimes overwhelmed him. The team knew it was not a matter of intelligence: Hayes was smart. They talked with him for hours before they signed him, and they went over the situations in which he was comfortable learning. He actually did grasp the offense when he was in the classroom. He put a lot of pressure on himself in games but often broke on routes too early, too late, or didn't go to the proper place at all. It was telling that he felt most at ease during a November 17 game at Oakland. He had no production that night. But he did have something that the rest of the offense had as well: a list of plays on his wristband.

After his admission in the *Globe* interview, Hayes caught one pass for the rest of the season. While the Patriots had been fortunate with free agents in 2001—Mike Vrabel, Antowain Smith, Larry Izzo, Roman Phifer—they were spotty in the same category in 2002. Fauria was excellent for them, both on the field and in makeup. A mason's son, Fauria learned about the sand-to-cement-to-water ratio when he was eight years old. He learned to make bricks and dig ditches. When he wasn't doing that, his father, Ashley, was telling him to either wash cars or do something that would put some grit under his fingernails.

The Patriots were casting about for *that* type of player,

and they had found such players in abundance the previous year. Their 2002 free market talent search, however, was frustrating and disappointing. Belichick respected Green's ability to make big plays, but he didn't like what he saw on film. He didn't like how long it was taking the safety to get to the ball. He was even more annoyed with a free agent defensive tackle named Steve Martin. Martin came advertised as a 320-pound run-stuffer. He didn't do that very well, although he was as glib as his comic namesake. He was one of the few Patriots who would approach reporters before reporters approached him. He had opinions on everything from the wealth of P. Diddy to the conundrum of Michael Jackson to the challenges facing an entrepreneur. He had attended the University of Missouri and was trying to run a restaurant in Columbia.

"This guy should be the fucking governor of Missouri," Belichick said of Martin during a coaches' meeting. The room had been dark earlier, and Belichick had control of the clicker. He was watching tapes of Martin in practice. "This is bad," the coach said. "This is just bad." He was already unhappy with the performance. The constant chattering and campaigning also sickened him, especially since the performance was so substandard. What made it worse was that the Patriots didn't have a lot of alternatives behind Martin. Belichick wasn't happy with what he was getting, but Martin did play in fourteen games. No one knew it on December 16, not even Belichick, but that would be the defensive lineman's last game as a Patriot.

"Last year" had been a familiar chorus among the Patriots and their fans—until the 24–7 loss to the Titans. "Last year" was seemingly the answer, question, and reference at the center of everything. A comment about the team's 5–5 start would often come with a companion piece: "They started 5–5 last year too." An observation about Smith's rushing yardage was usually paired with what he had done "last year." The Patriots' defense of 2001 had not been as soft against the run as the 2002 Patriots', but the "last year" choir was quick to recall that The Super Bowl XXXVI champions were not highly ranked on defense either. Everyone did it, and they did it daily. Belichick tried to shut himself and the team off from nostalgia, but it was difficult.

"It was so tough, because we had played a certain way the season before," Brady says. "We were still practicing hard, and competing hard. But we weren't winning. It was like, 'What the hell is the problem?' Coach Belichick was frustrated with the team a lot, and I was more stressed out than I had ever been. I thought it was very evident on my face. My body language was terrible for most of the year."

The nostalgia stopped in Nashville. Titans quarterback Steve McNair hadn't practiced all week because of sore ribs. But he was able to run for 49 yards and two touchdowns. Those 49 yards were the third-best number on the team after the 101 from Eddie George and 85 from Robert Holcombe. It was tough for any coach to watch and any team to experience. The Patriots were being bullied; the Titans refused to let them have the ball, holding it for a remarkable forty-one minutes and forcing the Patriots to squeeze any brilliance they had into a small space. But nothing was there.

It didn't matter that the Patriots knew the Titans were basically running Buddy Ryan's defense and that Ryan's son, Rob, was a New England coach. The staff knew what was coming: over front, man coverage, "46" package, blitz zone. Rob Ryan liked to joke that he and his twin brother,

Rex, drew up the defense, "showed it to Dad, and he called it the '46.' But he's not saying that." There was something the Patriots lacked, and what they lacked the Titans had. It was obvious to the nation's viewers, because one team—missing tackles, intercepting the ball and then fumbling it away, unable to avoid thoughtless turnovers—looked out of place standing next to the other. And if that wasn't bad enough, Brady had gotten hurt. The Patriots didn't say it, but it was a first-degree separation of his right shoulder—his throwing shoulder.

As he sat on the team's one A.M. charter flight back to Providence, Belichick thought about all the work they needed to do. When he told John Madden during the production meeting that the game would tell him a lot about his team, he had been hopeful, optimistic. Now there was just an inescapable sense of gloom and a true test of his leadership. They got back to Providence around four A.M. and were at the stadium shortly after five. Just in time to begin another day, another week, and another game with the New York Jets.

When the Patriots returned to Foxboro on Wednesday, December 18—Tuesday had been their day off—they were greeted by a large drawing near the bulletin board. It was a scale, with the logos of all the teams they had played in the past on one side and the green-and-white logo of the rival New York Jets on the other. The message was simple: the Jets were all that mattered.

The Patriots were 8–6. They could take a very direct route to the play-offs by winning their last two games, against the Jets and Dolphins. They would still be able to win by splitting the games, but that would put them in a maze of tiebreakers and mathematical possibility. It was easier to just win twice in two weeks.

It was the week before Christmas, but it was hard to know that in football operations. Downstairs the players and coaches were trying to figure out a way to beat the Jets, and upstairs the scouts were holding their early draft meetings. There wasn't a lot of joy after the Monday night loss to the Titans. Belichick wasn't in the mood for a lot of talking. He knew the Jets were not the same team the Patriots had beat in September, 44–7. Like Tennessee, New York had opened the season with a win and then lost four consecutive games. The Jets had a 2–5 record on October 28, but they were 7–7 as they prepared for their Sunday night game with the Patriots. Belichick clearly made those points at a noon meeting.

The next day he read some of the comments that Steve Martin had made to the New York media. Martin was a former Jet, so he was asked if he was surprised that his ex-teammate, All-Pro center Kevin Mawae, had been involved in a fight at practice.

"Yeah, I heard about that," Martin told the reporters. "That's what he does. He plays dirty. He used to do that when I was there. Someone probably got mad because he did something dirty. He did that the whole time I was there." Martin also reported that he was brought to New England to help out against the run and be effective on third down. But it appeared, he said, that his role had been reduced to standing around, since he had lost his starting job after the Patriots lost to Green Bay at home.

That week, Martin had lost his starting job. Now, before

the Jets game, he lost his employment altogether. He was fired three days before playing his old team.

Belichick was tired of him, for sure. He was also tired of being pushed around on defense. He was tired of the help-less feeling that mediocre teams have. It's the feeling that success is out of their hands, that some other team will have to come in for things to be right.

That feeling would become tangible fact on Sunday night. Later, in the off-season, Belichick would use the sec-ond New York game as a piece of evidence during an ani-mated speech in a coaches' meeting. This, he would argue, was why things had to change in Foxboro. He would point to poor coverage, particularly on third down. He would point to players' "giving up" opportunities to make tackles. He would note that quarterback Chad Pennington com-pleted his first 11 passes against the Patriots and, once again, another back—this time it was Curtis Martin—rushed for more than 100 yards.

The Patriots lost to the Jets, 30–17. And now, an hour af-ter the game, Belichick was in his office. His family and friends were either in the office with him or just outside, talking with each other. His parents were standing against a wall, a few feet away from the drawing of the "Jets scale," a drawing that was now moot. Belichick's mother, Jeanette, is a small woman who is as passionate about communica-tion as her son is about coaching. When she was in prac-tice, as she puts it, she spoke seven languages. In different ways—and in different places—she sometimes has the same analyses as her son. Once, on a trip home to see his parents in Annapolis, Belichick was giving some of the rea-sons for poor player performance. Near the top of his list was "shitty coaching." When he got home and was speaking with his mother in the kitchen, she gave her reasons why some students don't do well with foreign languages. "Bad teaching" was her quick answer.

She knew a lot more than languages. She knew football too. She turned to her husband and said, "You know what I don't understand? I don't understand why they don't call roughing the passer more. I thought Brady was going to be a bag of bones out there." Brady had completed just 19 of his 37 passes. He may have been hit well after he threw, but that wasn't why he was hurting. He still had discomfort from the shoulder injury in the Titans game. "I'm going to tell him that you feel sorry for him," Steve Belichick said to his wife. "I'm sure he'll be glad to hear that."

It was as if Steve Belichick were reading from a cue card. A couple of seconds after the comment was made, the lanky Brady turned the corner. He was walking slowly. His shoulders were slumped. He was well dressed—his sister Nancy likes to pick out the clothes he wears on game days—and he was wearing a floppy newsboy hat. Belichick's daughter, Amanda, was there with a friend, and they watched the handsome quarterback walk by. He looked to his left and recognized Steve and Jeanette. He leaned over to kiss the coach's mother. "They're killing you out there," she said. "They should call roughing the passer more." Brady blushed. He said he just wasn't playing well. He smiled at Amanda and her friend—a smile that excited the friend—and walked out to the players' parking lot.

It was well after midnight. Soon Belichick would step out of his office and walk down the hall. He had been rough on the team following the game, much tougher than he was after the loss to the Titans. He spoke to his friends. He stopped, briefly, next to his parents. His mother hugged him. "I love you," she said. Softly, he said, "You too."

A tough season had come down to one game. The Patriots would have to defeat the Dolphins and hope that the Packers could beat the Jets. If that happened, the Patriots and Dolphins would be 9–7, the Jets would be 8–8, and the Patriots would win the division on a tiebreaker. If not, the Patriots would simply fall back to being an average team, just one year after being the best team in football.

Late on Christmas night, a Wednesday, a snowstorm hit greater Boston. It had been raining earlier in the day, the rain turned to sleet, the wind blew—in some areas at sixty miles per hour—and about five inches of wet and heavy snow fell in Foxboro. It could have been the snow or it could have been the wind, but when the Patriots returned to work on Thursday, they found that their practice bubble was not usable. Because the bubble was at risk, the New England Patriots were going to have to take a road trip up Route 128 to Boston College.

A few players got a kick out of this as they saw three buses parked in front of football operations. "You mean to tell me that this organization can spend $325 million for a stadium," one of them said, "and they can't put out a couple of million for a new bubble?" Variations on that sentiment were expressed throughout the buses. (A new practice bubble would be in place for the 2003 season.) The Patriots arrived at Alumni Stadium, walked through the snow and ice, and entered the bubble. There appeared to be a baseball meeting going on at the end of the field. Belichick went to speak with the group, they applauded after a few minutes, and then they dispersed.

The field was free of kids, and that was a good thing. It was a parental advisory atmosphere. Weis yelled at rookie David Givens, who had dropped a pass against the Jets that could have turned the game. Belichick, who was still disgusted with his team's inability to cover, yelled at the defensive backs through coach Eric Mangini. "Hey, Eric," the coach shouted. "Why can't we cover anybody on 'Cover 5'? Someone is running free every fucking time. Every fucking time!" Mangini told his group to line up and try the coverage again.

The Patriots were injured—Tedy Bruschi and Deion Branch were out—and desperate. In a season that was nothing like the previous one, it seemed appropriate that they were in this position: on a college campus, in a bubble, competing for practice time with a group of baseball players. It would have been purely amusing if they had beaten the Jets. But in the context of the 8–7 season, the practice situation felt ridiculous.

When the session ended, the defending NFL champions returned to Foxboro to find ribs, cornbread, greens, and sweet potatoes in the cafeteria. For a little while their moods lifted. They had a good time together, as usual. They were a close team, something that Fauria had noticed as soon as he arrived in Foxboro.

"It wasn't like this in Seattle," he says. "I'll use training camp there as an example. There was a serving tray where they had the salad, and it was kind of like the divider in the room. There were tables on both sides. I'm telling you, all the white guys were on one side, and the black guys were on the other. Now, I'm not saying it was prejudice or a race issue, but it always seems to happen that way.

"I don't see that here at all. You see those domino games in the locker room? You have guys like Marc Edwards and Mike Vrabel saying, 'Slap the domino, motherfucker,' just like everyone else. Seriously, I think it's a credit to Scott [Pioli]. He really brings good guys in. And I felt that right away. All the guys are generally good guys, with the same emphasis on winning."

Belichick defined exactly what that emphasis was on Friday, in his most revealing production meeting of the season. Phil Simms and Armen Keteyian of CBS were at the meeting—Greg Gumbel would meet them later at practice—and they caught the coach in one of his unguarded moments. If it hadn't been so spontaneous, it would have seemed staged: Belichick flopped onto a brown coach and began joking with Simms and Keteyian. There were rumors about Bill Parcells joining the Cowboys, so Belichick jabbed Simms by asking if he was going to Dallas to be the offensive coordinator. Simms said he would love to coach if he could be well paid while not being accountable for a team's record. Everyone laughed.

The sight of Belichick on the couch was irresistible. "Are we your analysts?" Keteyian joked. He imitated a therapist. "So, Coach Belichick. Tell us how you feel. . . ." Simms told Belichick that he would have to pay for this session, and it was going to be expensive. "I'm just letting you know, Belichick: I'm going to charge your ass a lot of money." Eventually Bill on the Couch was asked if the Patriots had felt the weight of being Super Bowl champs. He was asked if the season had drained his team.

"I would never admit this publicly," he said. "But absolutely. There is so much pressure on this team. Every week. Every single week." Keteyian began reading off the Patriots' schedule to enforce the coach's point. "And even against Chicago," Belichick interrupted, "we went into their place while they were on a 6-game losing streak. It's been draining."

Belichick hadn't said anything like that all season to anyone in the media. He tried to find reasons that the Super Bowl didn't matter. He tried so hard that he may have ignored any hint of Super Bowl hangover. He had been trying to encourage the team to move on from something that not all of them—the rookies and free agents, for example— had experienced. But other teams weren't forgetting the Super Bowl. They were not going to let the Patriots creep up on them. They delighted in trying to clock the champions. And if the Patriots didn't treat the Miami game "like a wild-card play-off," as Belichick said in the production meeting, they were in their last days as champs.

At what was going to be the final Cabinet meeting of 2002—win or lose—Belichick reviewed the game plan at the Four Points Sheraton Hotel in Norwood. He had concerns about cornerback Ty Law's groin and asked Mangini about it. He wondered if the groin would become a problem during the game. Mangini said that Law would be shot up. "He won't miss this," Mangini said. Belichick reminded the coaches that the sun could be a factor. He compared it to the year before, when a pop kick had been sent toward a Dolphin, in hopes of getting a fumble.

He told Romeo Crennel that he didn't want to be too soft on first down. He told Weis that he wanted the Patriots to run against a seven-man box and beat man coverage. "There's not one play that doesn't do all that shit, as far as I can see," Belichick said. "Don't be afraid to throw it on first down. Things like 'X Option.' If those fuckers can cover us on that, it's going to be a long day."

It was one half of a long day on Sunday afternoon in Foxboro. The Dolphins were thirty minutes away from winning the AFC East, leading the Patriots 21–10 at halftime. The problems were not new: Ricky Williams, the NFL's leading rusher, already had 120 yards by halftime. The Patriots wanted to set the edge and force him back inside; Williams would sometimes dip inside and then bounce outside.

Outside linebackers coach Rob Ryan called one of his smartest players, Vrabel, on the sideline. "Vrabes," Ryan said, "I know Ricky is making it look like he doesn't wanna go outside. But I guarantee you he wants to. Don't let him do it."

It was the third quarter now, and the Patriots were beginning to do a better job on Williams. But they didn't have much time. They got an Adam Vinatieri field goal in the third to make it 21–13. But in the fourth, with eight minutes left, Brady threw a bad pass that was intercepted by Brock Marion. An Olindo Mare field goal with five minutes remaining made it 24–13. It certainly was looking like an 8–8 season for the Patriots.

They needed to do something quickly, so they went to a play that had been a part of their game plan the first time they opposed Miami, in October. On the call sheet that day the seventh item under "notes" read, "Pick on #21 in SUB (include GO's)." They were talking about cornerback Jamar

Fletcher. And everyone knew what GO meant. Go deep. "He doesn't have deep-ball speed and will struggle against faster receivers," read the Patriot scouting report. Givens, the rookie from Notre Dame, wasn't the fastest receiver. He did have an understanding of how to create separation, and he had earned the respect of his teammates with hard work. On first down at the Miami 33, Givens went on a GO route against Fletcher. He didn't catch the ball, but he did draw a pass interference penalty at the 3. One play later Brady threw across the middle to Troy Brown, who scored. When Fauria caught a 2-point conversion pass to make it 24–21, there was hope again.

There was the sense that Miami was gasping. There weren't even 180 seconds left, but that was plenty of time for the Dolphins to make mistakes. They guessed wrong on the kickoff—they thought it would be an on-side kick—and were out of position. So they started with the ball at their own 4. They had the lead, the Patriots were the ones who needed to stop the clock, and Miami had the NFL's leading rusher in their backfield. Yet, on the first two downs, they called for passes. When they did run, it was quarterback Jay Fiedler running, not Williams. Punter Mark Royals completed the disastrous series with a 23-yard punt.

The Dolphins had burned all of twenty-eight seconds.

New England actually got the ball to the Miami 25. But on third-and-1, Smith couldn't pick up the yard that would have given the Patriots the chance to go for the win in regulation. "Keep trying," Jason Taylor shouted in the direction of Belichick. The Dolphins defensive end was daring the coach to send Smith into the line on fourth down. "Keep trying," he repeated.

Instead, Vinatieri made a 43-yard field goal to tie it at

24. Eleven points in five minutes. Who didn't know what was going to happen in overtime? Who didn't know that there would be more Miami mistakes? The first was Mare kicking the ball out of bounds after the Patriots won the coin flip. Who didn't know that Vinatieri would win it with a 35-yard kick and then shrug later in the locker room, saying, "What can I say? This is what I do"?

Romeo Crennel called it early. He was watching the Green Bay–New York game, and he had an observation about the Packers. "Green Bay doesn't want to play today," he said. The Packers were already in the play-offs, and the Jets needed to win. The Jets were relentless too.

Brian Belichick was watching the game in his father's office. When Brett Favre threw a touchdown pass to former Patriot Terry Glenn, Brian had to tell his father. "Hey, Dad. Look who just scored: Terry Glenn!" They all gave each other high-fives and said what a dependable player (wink wink) the notoriously undependable Glenn was.

But it didn't matter. It was over. The Jets did whatever they wanted against the Packers. The final score was 42–17, and Crennel was right. Green Bay didn't want to play.

Belichick must have known it too. "I can't stay here and watch this," he said. He packed up some of his things and was gone by halftime, when it was still a 14–10 game. At least he didn't have to see the worst of it.

As he thought about it later that night and early the next day, he wasn't that angry about missing the play-offs. "It was probably for the best," he says. "It didn't look like we were going very far." He knew they would have had to go there without Brady, who had reinjured his arm against the Dolphins. He wouldn't have been available for a play-off game if there had been one.

But there wasn't. This was a team that had tried to be what it used to be. The lesson, though, was that none of us can go back. For one game, their last of the year, the Patriots were able to mimic themselves from 2001. By the time they got it right, December 29, 2002, it was far too late.

ROOKIES AND REPLACEMENTS

Only the naive didn't understand what the squad meeting truly represented. And no one in the Gillette Stadium auditorium, at least one season into a Patriots career, was considered naive. It was going to be good-bye for a dozen of them, maybe more. It was nine A.M. on December 30, the Monday morning after Miami. Just a couple of days earlier, in this same room, they had been asked to collectively figure out a way to beat the Dolphins. Now each of them was potentially an independent contractor who might be asked to turn in his ID card and work somewhere else.

Cold, yes. But each of them had gotten over cold a long time ago. This was what made them professionals: concentrating on doing a good job every day, even though the talent searchers in the

organization—the scouts—were in the same building trying to find people who could replace them. It was protocol,
not personal. And when the team had gone 9–7, it was
something else: inevitable.

So this was going to be the last meeting for several Patriots. They weren't going to be here on Saturday mornings
before a road trip, watching all the wives and girlfriends in
the parking lot wave to their men on the bus. No more
State Police escorts from two states—Massachusetts and
Rhode Island—on the way to T. F. Green Airport in Providence. Once there, the bus drives toward a security gate at
airport operations. It is waved through and pulls up to the
plane. No one is asking if you've packed all your bags yourself or if you talked to any strangers on the way to the airport. Just board the chartered plane—it's not a luxury
plane, it's just chartered—and wait for the flight attendants
to offer more food than necessary.

For some, this was going to be the end of hearing Belichick's raw analyses of the Patriots and the teams they
play. There would be no more surprises from the coach,
like the one he had after the Thanksgiving win in Detroit.
After leading the players in the Lord's Prayer, he told them
he had several announcements to make. It was all good
news. He was giving them the weekend off; that news drew
their applause. He told them to leave their red throwback
jerseys next to their lockers and to not even think about
keeping them. "By the way some of you guys look in these
red uniforms, don't gain too much weight," he cracked. He
told them that, with the weekend off, they should avoid
trouble. He glanced at Willie McGinest when he said "trouble," and McGinest started laughing. "Come on, Coach.
Why are you looking at me when you say that?" He asked

the players to give thanks and reminded them that there was someone they could call—a coach or family member—who had helped them along the way.

Next season, some of them were going to miss the camaraderie, adult and juvenile alike. They weren't going to be able to hear a few guys whistle on the plane as *The Godfather*'s Michael Corleone watched his Sicilian bride remove her shirt. In 2003, how many times would there be locker-room celebrations like the one in Champaign, Illinois? The Patriots had trailed the Bears by three touchdowns, 27–6, in the third quarter. They came back to win, 33–30, on a late touchdown catch by David Patten. "Where's the beer?" offensive lineman Grey Ruegamer shouted. "I've never met anyone luckier than Tom Brady," Mike Vrabel said so Brady, who had thrown 55 passes, could hear him. "If we had lost this game," Pepper Johnson announced, "it would have felt like losing to the University of Illinois! Because how can you lose to the Chicago Bears when you're not at Soldier Field? We're not even in Chicago."

It was fun. Now it was history. All kinds of practice conversations, weight-room competitions, observations about what was on the television in the cafeteria—all gone into the vault known as the 2002 season.

How long does it take to switch one's focus from one season to the next? How about one shift? The squad meeting was at nine o'clock. At four o'clock there was a "needs meeting" in Belichick's office. The coach, Ernie Adams, and Scott Pioli were all there with independent lists. They were charged with taking the first steps toward reconstructing the Patriots. It was going to take them from December 30, 2002, until August 19, 2003, to acquire and shape all the pieces they needed to be great again.

ROOKIES AND REPLACEMENTS

They weren't going to be able to do it alone. They were going to need help from ownership, the scouts, the assistant coaches, and in some cases the players themselves. They would do some work in Foxboro, but there would be trips to Mobile, Alabama, and Indianapolis as well. There was the East-West Game, the Cactus Bowl, the Senior Bowl, the Paradise Bowl, and the Hula Bowl. There was going to be pro free agency, a strange period: some players who didn't satisfy the Patriots would make another team happy, and some players who were fired by other teams would be embraced by the Patriots. All of those all-star bowls—not to mention the Super Bowl—were in January. The fifty-nine days of Pioli's January and February schedule were jammed with football activities. There was just one exception, at 5:20 in the evening on January 9: Pioli had a dental appointment, during which he was scheduled to have his teeth cleaned. He had to lead a department, watch film, consult with Belichick, and handle things at home with Dallas. She was four months pregnant with their first child.

It wasn't just the players. *Everyone* in the organization knew how unhappy Belichick was with the previous season. He became surly when anyone mentioned his secondary in a complimentary way. He was clearly going to overhaul it. He also wasn't going to tolerate any misevaluations by his coaches or by college or pro scouts. If you weren't going to be able to get it right, you were put on notice. He was coming after you. If you saw something positive and he didn't see it, it was okay. You just had better be prepared to defend it.

He gave Pioli, Adams, and all the coaches postseason assignments: they had ten games to watch, and they were

133

asked to make their evaluations off those ten games. They knew he would be watching too, and there was no such thing as a throwaway line when describing a player's strengths and weaknesses. If you said a player still had sudden burst, for example, and the coach didn't see it, he would ask you to cite your sources, like a professor demanding more from the bibliography. At the end of the year and well into January and wild-card weekend, it didn't feel like the Patriots had actually won nine games. This was the feeling that a six- or seven-game winner would have. From all perspectives, there was no confusion about what was starting to happen. In corporate-speak, there were going to be transfers, layoffs, firings, and vigorous interviewing of fresh-faced kids from college.

Anthony Pleasant had seen the ritual play out since 1992. Pleasant was a month away from his thirty-fifth birthday at the end of 2002. He was a deep man whom the players sometimes called "Moses" for his wisdom and religious convictions. He knew what was happening. He understood that he was at the age where it could happen to him, without anyone asking questions. "Sometimes the business takes the fun out of the game because of everything that goes on around you," he says. "You know, the different politics and that kind of stuff. So that takes the fun out of it and makes it hard to trust people. It's a coldhearted business. It's not the real world either. It's not the everyday nine-to-five job. It's a coldhearted, cutthroat business."

Larry Cook was one of the people assigned to find the best rookies and replacements for the Patriots. The scout didn't disagree with Pleasant's analysis. The nature of the job is diabolical. "You've got to be cruel at times," he says.

"It's a bit of a mercenary position." Cook has been involved with football evaluation for over forty years. He has seen the game from all regions of the country. He grew up on Chicago's South Side, went to college in Michigan, worked and taught in California, scouted nationally, and arrived in New England in 1985. He knew what Belichick wanted, and he knew how to think about what the coach wanted.

"A lot of times when a team gets to the Super Bowl, that's really the apex of their performance. And what you really have to guard against is becoming complacent with the personnel you have. When you do that, essentially, you step off the cliff. Our job is to have people in place, ready to be future Patriots. It may take them a year or two or three to develop—but hopefully not ten. We can't let the team fall off the cliff. That's the whole purpose of our job. That's what we have to prevent."

All of football operations went to work. Flights, hotels, and rental cars were booked. Sources were called. Office lights were left on a little longer than usual. They were all working for one of the most competitive coaches in the country, and they had to realize that he was angry. They had to realize that one thought was uppermost in his mind: the Patriots didn't even qualify for the right to guard their championship. At minimum, his next team had to be able to do that.

It was 7:15 on a Tuesday morning, and the temperature in Foxboro was in the single digits. On this windy day in January—the 22nd—Bill Belichick was taking a drive. He got behind the wheel of his Toyota SUV, slipped Santana's *Su-*

135

pernatural into the CD player, and started driving south toward Annapolis. He would see his parents and do some scouting at the University of Maryland. He would have his cell phone with him, and that was a good thing, because he had a lot of work to do.

As he drove through Rhode Island two things were apparent: he was tired—he had been rubbing his face and shifting in his seat—and he was agitated about his defensive backs. "We've got major problems in the secondary," he said. He wasn't happy with any of his safeties in 2002. He thought Victor Green had lost a lot of speed. He thought Lawyer Milloy had lost speed too, and he was shocked by the zeros Milloy posted in the playmaking categories—no forced fumbles, no fumble recoveries, no interceptions. Tebucky Jones missed too many tackles and was going to want a lot of money; Belichick had a problem with both of these things. He was surprised that on a defense ranked as low as the Patriots', the team had three starters make the Pro Bowl.

"I'm sorry," he said. "I just can't say anything good about our defense right now."

He said he was not sure what would be done about cornerback Ty Law's high cap number for 2003 or about Milloy's contract, which was backloaded. He needed to do something about his fatigue, though. He decided to take the next exit. He wanted to find a place where he could get a bottle of water. He gave no thought to his status as one of the most recognizable faces in New England. As soon as he stepped out of the car, a young man spotted him and yelled, "Bill, nice to see you." Belichick waved and walked into a convenience store, where four people stared at him as he brought the bottle to the counter.

ROOKIES AND REPLACEMENTS

Back on the road, his cell phone rang. It was Berj Najarian, the coach's executive administrator. Najarian had
earned Belichick's complete trust. ("No matter what I give
him, he can handle it. He's so competent. I wish I could be
as organized as he is.") Belichick was receiving an update
on strength coach Mike Woicik. The Jacksonville Jaguars
had faxed a request to speak with Woicik about becoming
their strength coach. Jack Del Rio, a close friend of
Woicik's, was the new head coach of the Jaguars. Najarian
told Belichick that the Patriots' chief operating officer,
Andy Wasynczuk, would be calling him soon.

Wasynczuk called a few minutes later, and Belichick already knew what to tell him about Woicik: "I'd like to give
him permission to speak with those guys, but I don't want
to give him permission yet to take the job. I'm not sure if
that's possible." And since they were on the subject of Jacksonville, Belichick mentioned that he wanted to hire former
Jaguars assistant John Hufnagel as quarterbacks coach.

He was working the phone and talking football. The
music changed from Santana to the Beatles to U2. Rhode
Island became Connecticut, and Connecticut became New
York. Belichick left a message for Robert Kraft so the
owner could be updated. He talked with Wasynczuk a second time. Somewhere on the New Jersey Turnpike he even
received a surprise phone call from a cousin who wanted to
set up a family reunion.

Soon enough he would have his own reunion, with
Mom and Dad. He wanted to take the scenic route into Annapolis, pointing out some of the local landmarks. He
smiled when he passed the restaurant on Dock Street
where he used to work. He was just 15 minutes away from
his parents' house; they have lived in the same place for the

past 44 years. Belichick has someone take care of their landscaping and was always making other efforts to modernize the home that they adored. Steve and Jeanette Belichick had been married so long, Jeanette says with a smile, "because I don't nag him." One of the few times that she did, she was right. She had been editing one of his football books, and she said she didn't understand the excessive jargon. "You're not supposed to understand it," he replied. "It's not for you. It's for football coaches." She shook her head. "That's the problem with you coaches. You're not thinking about the average reader." She was right. He accepted her changes.

Now she was at the door, wishing that her only child could stay longer than a day. She hugged and kissed him, told him to have a seat, and made sure she had all his updated numbers. And since it was Maryland, after all, she was making crabcakes. She is a calm woman who has a wonderful voice. She and Steve complement each other. He has a good sense of humor and doesn't mind telling you a few stories. He likes to sit in the family room, lined with books and game balls, and read the sports sections of the *Washington Post* and the local paper, the *Capital.* Sometimes when he can't believe something he's seen, he'll read it aloud to Jeanette to see what she thinks. When Belichick arrived at home, his father had been watching ESPN's *Pardon the Interruption.* "You ever watch this show?" he said to his son. "It's pretty good."

They are such good grandparents that their son ribs them sometimes. "Believe me," he said, "you want to be a grandchild in this house." Jeanette smiled. "Well, they're all good kids." She has pictures of them throughout the house, including a couple on the refrigerator. When Bill said that his son Stephen was going through a stage of being cool, Jeanette pointed out, "And *you* didn't think you were cool at the same age?"

It was a typical trip home, and they all wanted it to last longer. But it couldn't, and they all knew why. Belichick's parents saw that look on his face after the loss to the Jets— that game really stung him. As the wife of a coach and the mother of a coach, Jeanette understands the demands of building a team and then guiding it. Not much had changed. When he was sixteen, his mother could look at him and know what was on his mind. He is fifty now, and she does the same thing.

He would have breakfast in the morning and then get ready to head toward College Park. To think about self-scouting. To think about the tough but necessary decisions that needed to be made.

Before they can know what they need, they need to know who they are. This is one of Belichick's core philosophies, and it is why he was sitting in this Gillette Stadium room with a binder, notebook, pens, and pages of football statistics. All the coaches were there. Adams and Pioli were there. For a couple of days Kraft was there too.

This was a team evaluation meeting where no opinions were spared. It was just a bunch of smart guys talking football. But instead of a bar top there was a conference table. And rather than pure emotion—although there was emotion here—their conclusions were backed up with numbers, trends, and anecdotes. Every Patriots player was up for discussion. There were strengths and weaknesses for each one. There were comments and sometimes statistics on his mental errors, his performance in the weight room, his ability to be coached, his attitude, his ranking compared with others at his position leaguewide and his ability to help the team next year.

Emotionally, this was easier for Belichick to do than it was for the position coaches. The head coach was not dealing with a group of six to ten players to whom he may have grown close over the course of a season or two. Belichick didn't bring that type of closeness into it. He took the panoramic view. If he saw a weak spot from overhead, he was more likely to fix it aggressively. Business first. What he wanted to be able to gauge from these meetings, simply, was whether a player still was a good fit for the Patriots. If not, it was time to move on.

And it sounded as if everyone wanted to do that with young tackle Kenyatta Jones. He had made 23 mental errors—the highest number on the team—in 661 plays. His blocks graded out at 72 percent, the lowest on the team. His position coach was Dante Scarnecchia. If the Patriots had been a college, Scarnecchia would have been tenured. He has held a number of positions in his twenty years with the Patriots. Belichick respects him and takes his analyses seriously. Scarnecchia reported that Jones had poor practice habits, was late off the ball, and had questionable mental toughness.

"There are days when that guy comes out to practice and you just know that he ain't gonna fuckin' work," Scarnecchia said. He said that Jones's effort at Miami in October "was one of the worst ten-play stretches of any tackle in the league." Belichick agreed. "He killed us that day. There are stretches when he's just brutal." The only thing positive they could say about him was that he was young—twenty-four—and that he enjoyed facing good players. "He is your typical coach-killer," Charlie Weis said. "Most of his teammates have no confidence in him. All of the offensive linemen know he can't be counted on, and the quarterbacks know it as well."

They still weren't done with him.

Scarnecchia reasoned that Jones may have had a self-image problem. "Not to get too fuckin' psychological here," he said. He then questioned his own coaching, wondering whether he should show some restraint and not ride Jones so much. "But," he concluded, "that would be very hard."

Most people in the room—including new quarterbacks coach Hufnagel—realized that Jones was the baseline. They realized that no other player they evaluated was going to fall below that level. If so, nonplay-off seasons were going to be the norm.

The entire tone of the conversation changed when it was time to evaluate guard Damien Woody. Scarnecchia liked him. Woody had made just 6 mental errors in 957 plays. He graded out at 89 percent on all of his blocks, the highest number on the team. "He's tough," Scarnecchia said. "He's competitive. He's durable. He's good in meetings. He accepts challenges." Belichick added that Woody was tough. He said more players like the team's third-round pick in 2001 could learn from his pain threshold. "Brock Williams *still* hasn't recovered from a high-ankle sprain," Belichick said with a smirk, referring to the former Patriots cornerback.

On some players, these men could sort through the information without much of a debate. Some players they just saw the same way. They all agreed that they needed to find a way to get the ball to Kevin Faulk more often. And that the drop in Antowain Smith's forty times—from 4.44 in 2001 to 4.54 in 2002—was a concern. "I'm worried about it," Belichick said. Weis concurred: "This was a shitty year. He would let some slapdick corner come up and tackle him after he gained one yard." They loved Matt Light's improvement from year one to year two. As a rookie left tackle, he had made 35 mental errors in 769 plays. His second year was much cleaner: 12 errors in 1,030 plays.

A few of them questioned the toughness of Patrick Pass, who could play on special teams and at fullback. "This guy gets a hangnail and you think you have to call the mortuary. He's dead," said Brad Seely, the special-teams coach. Weis said there were lots of phrases for guys—coach-killer, enigma—and all of them described Pass. "The only thing in his defense—and believe me, I can't stand the motherfucker—is that the quarterbacks like him. They ask me, 'What about Pass?' I don't know why."

Belichick jumped in with an idea: "Let's try to run him off and see if he responds to that." Ernie Adams said Pass was a good guy to make an example of and that it was time to ship him out.

The strongest reaction of the day shouldn't have been a surprise to anyone. The subject was defense, and Belichick had a real problem with some of the comments about linebacker Ula Tuitele. The problem was that the comments were positive and Belichick didn't want to hear it. You could tell that he was on edge and that this wasn't about Tuitele as much as it was desperation to improve a defense that couldn't defend itself. This wasn't about Tuitele as much as it was a late response to Pepper Johnson's comment that Larry Izzo had the potential to be "a Bill Romanowski–type player." Izzo was a Pro Bowler on special teams; Romanowski was one of the top "SAM" or strong-side linebackers in the league. "That's a reach," Belichick had told Johnson. Now he had to hear several coaches praise Tuitele. It was too much for him to handle.

"I don't know if we're seeing the same guy," he said. He asked Josh McDaniels to turn out the lights. He went to the Pinnacle system, a computerized library that contains every play that a coach can dream of watching. If you want to see all the team's plays that begin from the left hash mark on third down, you can do it. The system helps keep track of trends—percentage of plays run left, right, and up the middle—and it helps a coach better understand a player's strengths. Belichick wanted McDaniels to show some clips of Tuitele. What he saw didn't impress him. "The guy is slow as shit," he said. "I don't see how we get faster on defense with guys like this on the field. He wasn't blocked. He just can't run." There was going to be a twenty-minute break coming up, because now Belichick was about to explode: "I'm tired of thinking our team is good against Detroit, Buffalo's horseshit offensive line, and Philly's third-string offense. I don't give a fuck about that. We're one of the bottom five teams defensively in the league. We suck at stopping the run. We're bad in the red area. And we can't get off the field on third down."

It was time for that break. No one needed to guess where the Patriots would be looking in free agency and the draft.

FINDING THE
MISSING PIECES

There aren't many people who better understand Belichick than Scott Pioli. This is what happens when your boss doubles as a best friend: you know when he is venting, and you know when he truly wants something drastic to happen. You know when he is being reasonable, and you know when he is being unfair because of a bad day. You know some of his football catchphrases like "That's not what we're looking for" and "It doesn't get any worse than that" and "Look at this asshole" (which is sometimes intended as a compliment).

Pioli has seen Belichick's growth as a father, husband, manager, and coach. If Pioli were given 20 random questions and told to answer them as Belichick might, he wouldn't embarrass himself with his responses. He knew, without it being said, that his department would have to have its best year. He and his scouts were going to be reshaping the infrastructure of the team. They were going to be evaluating players and recommending that the Patriots either draft or sign some of them. As a friend, Pioli knew how much the 9–7 season had hurt Belichick. As an employee, he knew he was going to have to do something to prevent the hurt from recurring. So when Pioli enters the second-floor conference room and listens to the opinions of his scouts, he is carefully considering every point. He is an intense listener and note-taker. There are times when the scouts are reading their early draft reports aloud and they glance at Pioli to see if he has any reaction. For a moment they are all back in junior high, trying to satisfy a teacher with a probing eye and a red pen.

Pioli usually is at the front of the room for these sessions. He sits in a black chair, tilting and listening. He has copies of their reports in binders, and his pens and highlighters are not far away. Away from here, his jokes are always good and his one-liners come as often as blinks. (Nancy Meier, a personnel administrator who has been with the Patriots since the mid-1970s, says Pioli's wit reminds her of a former New England coach. That coach happens to be Pioli's father-in-law, Bill Parcells.) Away from here, he has been known to ask younger members of his department about slang, wanting to know the difference between "bling-bling" and "ice." But this place—which morphs into the draft room for one weekend each April—is where he often points out inconsistencies, oversights, and sloppiness. He circles in red and writes, "What are you saying?" or "What does this mean?" or "This is weak."

It is not always about wanting to be right—he will be the first to tell you that he shouldn't have pushed for the signing of Eric Bjornson or the drafting of Jabari Holloway. For Pioli, it is about being thorough so that his department can hold up its end of the deal with Belichick. The coach wants players who can fit in or adjust to his system. Pioli is responsible for making sure his men know what that system is, can communicate in that system, can make comparisons to other players who have been or are in the system, and can ultimately recommend players who might replenish the system and reject those who don't.

Belichick didn't have a winning record for four of his five seasons in Cleveland. Although several factors contributed to the mediocrity—inheriting an awful team in the pre–free agency era and the unprecedented distraction of an owner moving a franchise *during* the season—poor drafts and poor signings were part of the problem as well. Pioli witnessed it himself. In his midtwenties then, he was there with Belichick in the early 1990s, a Browns employee with little money—he wouldn't order cable TV because it was too expensive—and no authority. He saw the way low-character, high-maintenance players could deplete a team. He saw how a low-performing team could turn a city and organization against you. Because of that, he understood why no one really stops thinking about security in this business. Moments after the Patriots won Super Bowl XXXVI in New Orleans, Pioli and his wife lay on their bed in the Fairmont Hotel. As a raucous party began in the Imperial Ballroom, Dallas Pioli looked at her husband and said, "We're safe for another year."

He agreed. It's not like a championship is worth a lifetime of grace and immunity. This is part of the reason mistakes haunt him, even though he can walk down the hallway and see photos and mementos of Super Bowl bliss. Some people have photographic memories. Pioli's memory is a leather-bound photo album, going all the way back to Little League in Washingtonville, New York, in 1972. He played for a team called the Royals then, and their record was 2–13. The losses upset him so much that his parents threatened to remove him from the league. He still doesn't lose well. It is yet another thing he and Belichick have in common. They don't put their feet on tables and reflect on their greatness. They are analysts, stalking themselves for loopholes and weaknesses. When they find them, especially in retrospect, they want to perform autopsies on the errors so they won't happen again.

In the Jabari Holloway case, for example, Pioli says he should have trusted his instincts. The tight end from Notre Dame made him nervous as soon as Pioli found out why he was late for practice.

Chemistry class.

"By your senior year, football had better be a priority if you're going to be an NFL player," he says. "And I don't care about chemistry labs. You know what? You can come back and get your grades. To me that explained that something larger was going on. That there were other things in life clearly more important than football. He could have done it some other way where it didn't interfere with his football. That bothered me."

The Patriots drafted Holloway with their second fourth-round pick in the spring of 2001. He didn't last long. The team drafted a tight end, Daniel Graham, in the first round in 2002. Holloway was released and signed by the Houston Texans.

This is how a segment of the Patriots' program works. It is driven by a concept that is rare not only in sports but in American society. The idea, in a country full of social and entertainment options, is that the obligations of the job—and devotion to and mastery of the job—are an employee's top priority. The Patriots are attempting to stack their roster with productive players who either think that way now or are on the cusp of a conversion. They don't want to be paternalistic figures asking their players, "Did you put in extra film time?" They want the kind of players who want to do it without being asked.

"I'm looking at it from an employer's standpoint," Pioli says. "What else is this player going to have in his life that's more important than football, other than a chemistry lab? I can't always put my values onto people. But here is what I know: my job is to find players for a head coach who wants football to be the most important thing in their worlds. I believe in it.

"I miss time with my family, my wife. Bill misses time with his children. Not that football is more important, but we've got a job to do. Football is going to pay a kid a minimum of $200,000 or $225,000 a year as soon as he gets out of college. There's summer courses to pick up grades; there's the spring semester."

Pioli's opinions, like Belichick's, are so clear and blunt that there's little if any room for misunderstandings. In fact, it's written in the manual that all scouts must have a clear opinion. Neutrality or passive-aggressiveness can get you fired. You actually get credit when you logically disagree with the boss. "I want them to know their opinion is important," says Pioli. "As a matter of fact, it's so important that part of the evaluation of you is going to be whether or not you have one."

Pioli isn't the only one who realizes what is at stake prior to the 2003 draft. His scouts do as well, and they don't lack opinions. They talk for hours so they can come to some agreement on a player. They talk about every aspect of a player, from his body type to his favorite movie. They have conversations about wide butts, big butts, high cuts, large thighs, barrel chests, big bones, and stiff hips. Scout Jake Hallum describes a player as having a "wood hauler's ass"—which is good. One former Patriots scout, Jason Licht, describes a player as being "stiffer than a wedding dick"—which is not good.

They talk about diets: "I'm telling you, Scott. This kid has always had poor eating habits. This kid has a sensitive stomach. I don't know if you've talked to his people."

They talk about lifestyles: "In reference to his marijuana use, I'm positive that he has used in the past. . . . I know that football is important to this guy. I don't think he's a dumb kid. We were talking about football, and he seemed to have a pretty good grasp of it. He doesn't really care about school; he wants to be a football player."

They talk about character: "He's a book-smart guy. He had some accountability problems early in his career with his classes and labs and stuff like that. He wouldn't call over and let 'em know what was going on. So he would be late for stuff, but they got all that straight. And he hasn't had a problem since."

One floor above the cafeteria, they talk about the prospects who might replace a few players who are eating below: "As far as Marc Edwards goes, I don't think this kid has the versatility that Edwards has in our system. I know that Charlie [Weis] likes to split him out a little bit and leak him into the flat. I thought this kid was a little too stiff to be able to do that. I do think he's a draftable guy, and I think he could help us in our running game."

They talk about their own waffling: "You know, I guess as we move along here we're going to have to nut up here and decide."

Pioli has no problems staying objective in most of these discussions, but sometimes he lends his personal experiences to balance the arguments. The characterization of one player as "aloof" and "not overly bright" gets his attention.

"Are the people at the school saying he's not smart?" he asks. "The guy's got a 22 test, which isn't bad. Is it just because he's—"

"No, no," the scout interrupts. "Mathematically he's okay. But he has no communication skills. He's not a communicating type, but he can pick up numbers. So—"

"This guy goes five years of school and gets in trouble one time. I'm saying, let's not kill him on that. Let's not ignore it, but let's not kill him on it. The other thing is, he's a Detroit kid. Let's not kill him because of the way he speaks either. Do you remember A. P. in 1992?"

"A. P." is Anthony Pleasant, a player who may not have become an All-Pro but who had a significant impact on Pioli personally. Pleasant grew up in Century, Florida, a classic one-stoplight town on the Florida-Alabama border. He went to college at Tennessee State, arriving there as a six-foot-five-inch, 208-pound defensive end. Pioli understands that if someone chooses to focus on or be distracted by Pleasant's deep southern accent, that person is missing a gem. He understands that the Pleasant story has to be a part of scouting because the Patriots' type of player can't be based purely on numbers.

The scouting manual emphasizes leadership in some areas. How many players would be confident enough to gather all the black players around him in training camp and say, "Do you hear white guys calling themselves 'honkies'? No. So why do we call each other 'niggas'? When are we gonna grow up? There ain't nothing positive about that word at all. From now on, we ain't gonna have that word used in here no more."

Pleasant did that with the Patriots and got immediate results.

Ten years earlier, in 1994, he began to change the way Pioli thought about spirituality. The Browns were returning from a December trip to Dallas. Pioli noticed that Pleasant was reading the Bible, and the men began to converse about it. They talked about creation versus evolution and the big bang theory. This went on for the remainder of that trip and several times afterward. Pioli would pose philosophical questions to Pleasant, and Pleasant would give spiritual answers. If Pioli stumped him on something, Pleasant would research and return with an answer that satisfied him. Eventually Pioli went to church with Pleasant. Toward the end of the service the preacher made an altar call, inviting anyone to come forward for individualized prayer.

"The first time that happened, he said he just got in a cold sweat," Pleasant says. "You know, he said he couldn't move. He came back another Sunday, and he said, 'I'm going up this time.' He went, and I could see how relieved he was. Now, I hope he can have an impact on this organization. I hope he will continue to grow and not be ashamed of his faith."

Scout discussions can go on for at least eight hours a day during some of the draft meetings. And it's not like these scouts aren't used to long days. All of them have sat in offices for hours, watching film. They have been on the road for two weeks at a time, football drifters who absorb as much information as they can before moving on to State College or Lincoln or Corvallis. The best ones have developed sources at each stop. They chat with head coaches as well as cops. They pay attention to strength coaches, trainers, graduate assistants, and third- and fourth-stringers who watch the stars when the stars may be oblivious to them. They often check into their hotels at eight or nine P.M. They power their laptops shortly after that, catching up on reports that will be sent back to Foxboro. If they had time to hold court in sports bars, they'd be the brainiacs of any joint in the country. That's the case for dozens of scouts around the league. A few of them who work for one of the national services—National Football Scouting and Blesto—are amused at draft time. They can see their verbatim reports in football magazines because, presumably, one among them has sold the reports to an agent.

The Patriots are one of four teams with no affiliation to either National or Blesto. Their scouts are supposed to have the football skills to recognize talent and the journalistic skills to find untold stories. They are respectful and relentless when they are on the nation's campuses. They play by a school's rules, but they are resourceful enough to find the answers they need.

"Let's say you and I are scouting and we're at Virginia today," says Licht, who was a trusted Patriots' evaluator until he left for Philadelphia after the 2003 draft. "You might be close friends with the defensive backs coach. He's going to tell you things that he's not going to tell me. So I'm going to try to dig to get that information. But in the end I know he's not telling me the whole . . . he's not lying, but he's not telling me what I want to hear. He's not addressing some of the concerns I have. My job as a scout is to find it out. Whether that's trying to take you out for drinks, getting it out of you that way. Or giving you something so you give me something back. Every scout has his own little way of doing it."

Bobby Grier, who hired Licht in 1999, oversaw the Patriots' scouting system before Pioli did. Grier made nine first- and second-round draft picks between 1997 and 1999. Just one of the nine picks, Kevin Faulk, is still with the team. The Patriots began to rot in those years, from their talent to their salary cap to their spirit. Grier and former head coach Pete Carroll—a pair who did not vacation together on Nantucket as Pioli and Belichick do—took the brunt of the blame and lost their jobs because of it. Their scouting philosophy was different from this one.

"Your balls weren't on the line if a guy didn't make it," Licht says. "It was clear that the scouts were telling them who the players were and they were going to make the decisions. Bill and Scott make the decisions now. But your balls are on the line if you say a player isn't going to be a problem off the field. If he is, then it's your fault. You're responsible for the players the Patriots draft. You're not responsible for how players turn out somewhere else.

"If I said a guy was a first-round pick, the Colts picked him, and if he turned out to be a bust, they wouldn't have looked down on me. They wouldn't have said I was a bad grader. Because that player in the *Patriots'* system might have been successful."

Pioli reads all the things the scouts have written and listens to many of the things they have to say. During a meeting he knows whom to push in front of everyone and whom to pull to the side. It is a diverse group. Pioli has known his director of college scouting, Tom Dimitroff, since Cleveland, when he worked with Dimitroff's father. In this environment of long days and fast food, Dimitroff may be the only vegetarian in the league. Kyle O'Brien is the young scout from Harvard. Hallum is an expert on southern sayings and offensive linemen. Lionel Vital is the former NFL and Canadian Football League player who sometimes acts out the words on his reports. When "L. V." says a lineman has strong hands, he clenches to illustrate. Larry Cook is the former driver's ed teacher with an instructor's sense for something amiss. Cook was skeptical when he watched former UCLA quarterback Cade McNown work out—and scrape to find receivers to catch the ball for him. That was when he knew there must be a story with McNown and his teammates. And there was a story. When the Bears drafted McNown in the first round, there were some scouts who were uneasy with the pick. The Bears would soon find out why: McNown developed a reputation as a quarterback who was not tough enough or accountable enough to be a great starter.

The Patriots scouts' knowledge of the system, originally

created by men like Bucko Kilroy and the late Dick Steinberg, is essential. Pioli and Ernie Adams wrote in new material and tweaked some of the old information to make it precisely for Belichick's Patriots. You have to know the book and system terminology. Have to. You never know, as Licht learned one Friday afternoon in October 2002, when a random quiz is coming. He walked by Belichick's office on his way to his own. The coach asked if he could talk to him about "a few guys." Fifty players later, Licht was still answering Belichick's questions.

"And then, while you're talking, he's typing notes into his computer," Licht says. "And he'll say, 'Yeah, yeah. I saw this guy versus Penn State. He's just kind of flopping around. I don't think that's our type of guy.'"

"Our kind of guy" is someone who can be quantified. The Patriots' grading system for players has its own music and melody. It is the marriage of science and art, instinct and intellect. There is a New England alphabet and New England numerology. Every player who puts on a silver helmet is defined in these terms.

First, there is a twelve-letter lowercase alphabet. These are known as "alerts." A lower-case "a" does not stand for excellence; a player gets that if there are concerns about his age, either too young or too old. A "c" is for a character concern. An "x" is for an injury problem. A "t" is someone who will make special-teams coach Brad Seely happy, while a "tt" is a special-teamer so good—someone on the level of a Steve Tasker or a Bennie Thompson—that he can make the roster for his teams ability alone. A report, for example, reading "6.50ly" should be clear to everyone: that's an overachiever who is a "Make It+" player, which is a solid pro. He is a transfer student, which means the scouts had better have the inside details of why he transferred from his previous school. Putting a "y" on a player lets Pioli know that there has been a transfer. The "l" alert is for someone who finished his college career at a lower level of competition, either Division 1-AA, Division 2, or Division 3.

The scouts also use thirteen letters in the upper-case alphabet, although you can double or triple the letters in some cases to make your point. The top two letters—"A+" and "A"—mean what you would expect them to mean. If Pioli and Belichick see those letters on a report, they know they are looking at a player who will be wearing a yellow jacket and giving a speech on the steps of the Pro Football Hall of Fame. A "Q" is a rare player who happens to be height-deficient. "C" is for some circumstance—it could be anything—that has restricted a very good player's production. A "P" is for players such as Adam Archuleta of the Rams and Mike Vrabel and Tedy Bruschi of the Patriots. They are top projection players who are being counted on to play a position in the pros that they didn't in college. Bruschi was a defensive lineman at Arizona who became a linebacker with the Patriots. Vrabel was an All-Conference defensive end at Ohio State who became a linebacker, first with the Steelers and then in New England.

"Just remember," Pioli said in an early draft meeting, "Bill can do things with 'P' types if they're good enough. We've got two starting linebackers that are projection players."

When the scouts are asked to put a player into a specific box, they have eight groupings from which to choose:

1. Starter: 9.00–9.99 A+, 8.00–8.99 A, and Q (height-deficient) 8.00–8.99

2. Circumstantial Starter—a first-year NFL starter whose production has been restricted by some circumstance, which may include an NCAA rules problem, problems with an agent, or a personal or family conflict: C7.00–7.99
3. Make It +—a player who is not expected to start in his first season but is expected to contribute in year one and eventually develop into a starter: 6.50–6.99
4. Dirty Starter—could start, but something about the player is restrictive (maybe not enough speed or athletic ability); the manual says this could be the category for over- and underachievers: 6.00–6.49
5. Make It—a backup who won't win or lose a game for you: 5.50–5.99
6. Free Agent—not expected to make the team but could rise to the "Make It" level with time in NFL Europe or on the practice squad: 5.00–5.49
7. Pats Reject—a reject by Patriot standards, but could land somewhere else in the NFL: 4.90–4.99
8. Reject—doesn't belong in the NFL: 1.00

Three dimensions of a player—major factors, critical factors, and position skills—are graded on a scale from 1 to 9: 1, according to the manual, is a "reject," and 9 is that Hall of Famer. Highlighted in red, atop the grading chart, is a reminder: "The key number is 6. . . . If a player is 6 in any factor or skill, we will be satisfied with his performance of this skill or critical factor. He is not going to dominate. However, this is a solid level of performance or competence. This is the type of grade that leads a player to the 'Make It+' level."

Major factors are the same for all positions. All players are judged in seven categories: personal/behavior, athletic ability, strength and explosion, competitiveness, toughness, mental/learning, and injury/durability. The categories in critical factors and position skills are in flux, depending on the position.

During the amending and rewriting of the book, the Patriots sketched a silhouette of a quarterback and unknowingly came up with a Tom Brady portrait. "It fits him to a T," Pioli says. The book says several things about what a quarterback for the Patriots must be, but four of them stand out:

1. "Be the mentally toughest and hardest-working player on the team."
2. "Be able to take a big hit and then walk into the huddle and call the next play."
3. "Have his head screwed on straight enough to handle the pressure and scrutiny to which all NFL QB's are subjected. (A Ryan Leaf fiasco can cripple a franchise for years.)" ("You couldn't get anyone to say anything nice about Ryan Leaf when he was leaving," Pioli elaborated one day in his office. "His teammates were happy to see him leave Washington State. He was an asshole.")
4. "If you want to know who the good quarterbacks are, watch the passes they complete under a heavy rush. Watch the first downs they get on third and long, passing into heavy coverage.

Listen to what their teammates have to say about them." (The previous quote is from an athlete whom Brady grew up imitating and to whom he is often compared—Joe Montana.)

The descriptions are perfect. What he doesn't understand, Brady teases, is that "they waited so long to take me. Come on. One hundred and ninety-nine?"

The Patriots got lucky with Brady. He shouldn't have been available to them nearly two hundred picks into the draft. In one sense, the Brady selection is a wonderful story. It allows football fans to forever claim that championships can be won without a highly selected quarterback. But then, the Brady story can also be perceived as an understated evaluation. If the Patriots knew what he could be, they would have never taken Adrian Klemm and J. R. Redmond before him. Going into the 2003 off-season, the Patriots couldn't have—as silly as it sounds—any Brady episodes. They would need to recognize the most talented players early, and try to select them. But before they could select them, they had to travel to Indianapolis. There, the entire league would engage in the annual ritual that comes before selection. That would be the scouting combine or, frankly, inspection.

THE MEAT MARKET

In the weeks before Indianapolis, Pioli, Belichick, Larry Cook, and Jason Licht had begun to develop an occasional routine. They would meet in the draft room, before the early draft meetings, and shuffle some magnetic names on their tentative draft board. Although Belichick's displeasure with the defense was by now well known in the building, he concentrated on all positions.

After they had analyzed a player, they would line up the board. This was based on two things: the prospect's grade according to the team's grading system, and the prospect's skills compared to people already on the team.

For example, the Patriots had high grades for USC safety Troy Polamalu. They put one of their positive alerts on him—"tt"—to indicate his exceptional special-teams ability. It wasn't enough to say, "Po-lamalu is good." The more precise question became, "Do you like Polamalu more than Lawyer Milloy? How much better is he than Tebucky Jones?" And so on. The magnetic strip was then placed on the board accordingly. If there was a lingering uncertainty about a player, his name was tilted on the board, a reminder that there needed to be more discussion or investigation.

The strip now told more of a story: you knew where the player ranked among his college peers, and you could see where he projected as a player with the Patriots.

It was critical for Pioli and Belichick to have a sense of their preliminary board before Indianapolis. Lots of things were certainly going to change between February and April. But they still needed to have a plan for how they were going to approach the NFL's annual job fair. They were going to have a meeting on February 17, the day before the combine, to talk about pro free agents. What was the sense of going to Indianapolis and devoting an inordinate amount of time to, say, linebackers when that would be a free agency priority? (Yet, they had had a January 31 deadline for submitting a list of players they wanted to interview at the National Invitational Camp, which is what the combine is formally called. By the time the Patriots actually interviewed some of the people on their list, their interest in those players had changed—for better or worse.)

They had already identified the man they wanted most in free agency. While fans and draftniks had them selecting everyone from Boss Bailey to E. J. Henderson to Gerald Hayes, the Patriots knew the player they needed was already in the league. It was Rosevelt Colvin of the Bears, a twenty-five-year-old outside linebacker with pass rushing skills. Colvin was considered one of the top free agents available. Belichick had an insider's scouting report on him because one of his best friends in the league, Jerry Angelo, was the Bears' general manager.

It wasn't going to stop with Colvin. In the needs meeting the day after the season, a "Star" defensive back—one who matched up in the slot—was discussed. Belichick didn't like what his team did on third down, and he didn't think Terrell Buckley was as physical as he needed to be to play inside. So the Patriots were going into free agency and the draft looking for two types of corners—insides and outs. They had two picks in the first round—numbers 14 and 19—and they already knew they were likely to hold on to the first one and draft a defensive tackle.

Maybe the plan was loose, but they could travel to Indianapolis with it.

No other professional sport has anything resembling the combine. It is a week of probing and testing, gawking and prodding. The players are asked to strip to their shorts and told to look straight ahead and then turn to the side as they are videotaped. They walk around with assigned numbers and groups, which seem to be just as important as first names. The interviews sometimes seem more like interrogations. The Crowne Plaza at Union Station is the hotel transformed into a league compound.

Teams can submit up to sixty players they'd like to speak with, for fifteen minutes at a time, in their private rooms. There is a horn for the start of the interviews, and a horn signaling their end. The system was instituted because in the "free market" teams would fight over players, arguing that they had gotten to the prospect first. And silly games would be played, like a team sending attractive young women to escort players to its headquarters.

That's unnecessary in the new system. All of the talking is scheduled. It is up to the coaches, scouts, and general managers to draw out the information they most want to hear.

"Everybody in the NFL is dealing with the same names," says Cook. "It's like a lot of things. When you go to a bar at night, that girl appeals to you. But that one over there, argh, she's ugly. The next guy thinks she's pretty cute. It's all in the eye of the beholder. We're looking at the same numbers, the same math, the same measurables. But we all have different takes on what it means."

As the Patriots welcomed players into their Crowne Plaza suite, they were focusing mainly on character and intelligence. They are good interviewers, mostly because they are prepared. Sometimes they ask a player if there is anything in his background that they should know about, even if they already know about it. Their repertoire of interviewing techniques is diverse: good cop–bad cop, sympathetic listener, wiseass. Pioli and Cook are almost always in the room. Coaches usually come in when players at their positions are being interviewed. They rarely leave an interview not knowing how they feel about a player.

When Illinois receiver Brandon Lloyd came in, he was asked why he was choosing to do an online "diary" of the combine. "David thought it would be a good idea," he said, speaking of his agent, David Dunn. They nodded. Fifteen minutes later Weis had a one-liner for the road: "Enjoy your writings now, because when we draft you we're going to tell you to shut the fuck up."

Boss Bailey, the linebacker from Georgia, impressed them with his honest analysis of his game. The scouts had said a few weeks earlier that Bailey missed too many tackles by overrunning plays. That was exactly what he said about himself.

They were thoroughly entertained by receiver LaTarence Dunbar of Texas Christian and defensive end Alonzo Jackson of Florida State. Dunbar was confident and full of energy, excited to talk with Seely about special teams. He mentioned his kickoff returns for touchdowns so often that Seely said, "Now wait a second. Are these different touchdowns or are you talking about the same ones?" Jackson walked around the room and shook hands with everyone. When he saw Romeo Crennel, he said, "This is the man, right here. The defensive coordinator, the man I need to see."

Some players who came into the room were humble. Some, like Ohio State safety Mike Doss and Notre Dame safety Gerome Sapp, knew where everyone was supposed to be when Crennel quizzed them on defense. Some couldn't articulate their own assignments in their college schemes. Some, like Pittsburgh defensive back Torrie Cox, acknowledged their mistakes and gained the respect of the Patriots. Cox said he once got into a fight with former teammate Antonio Bryant. The coaches paid attention then, because Bryant's demeanor had turned them off the year before. "So why'd you fight him?" Cox was asked. He replied, "That mouth of his. Sometimes that mouth of his gets to be too much." There was laughter followed by, "Torrie, you just went up a notch in our eyes." Some players just lied about their skirmishes.

Across the street from the hotel, players worked out at the RCA Dome. Belichick sat high in the Dome seats watching the workouts, but he didn't put a lot of stock in what was happening on the field. A lot of other teams didn't either. They were more interested in the exhaustive medical testing. Anyway, workouts were becoming so rare at certain positions—like running back—that Derek Watson of South Carolina State got an ovation just for running the 40.

Belichick and Pioli spent some of their time catching up with friends around the league. Pioli had breakfast with his father-in-law, Bill Parcells. Belichick talked with Super Bowl–winning coach Jon Gruden of Tampa Bay. "I wrote an article about you in the *New York Times*," Belichick said. "Did you see it?" Less than a month earlier, a Belichick column headlined "O.K., Champ, Now Comes the Hard Part" appeared on the *Times* op-ed page. It was a thirty-seven-point essay on what to expect after winning the Super Bowl. "I didn't see it," Gruden said. "I want to check that out, man." Chicago head coach Dick Jauron, who played for Belichick in Detroit, stopped by. The three of them talked and laughed near the field entrance of the Dome. They all have had to play versions of The Game with the media, so it was strange to see them as their relaxed selves: wearing jeans and sweatshirts and sneakers and enjoying a football atmosphere.

All of them had an idea of what players they liked. No one said anything about it. Or if they did, it was a test to see the others' reaction. Belichick did have a few light moments with two members of the Oakland Raiders. He started to say hello to Al Davis and kept walking, and Davis said, "Don't even think about walking by me. Come over here." He and Raiders general manager Mike Lombardi, Belichick's former personnel director in Cleveland, talked about what they would do to get New York Jets receiver Laveranues Coles on their team. "I'd give up our second-rounder for him," Belichick said. "Hey, I'd give up one of our firsts," Lombardi answered. (Washington, though, just gave up money by signing Coles to a free agent contract.)

In between trips to St. Elmo's Steakhouse—where Belichick devoured the shrimp cocktail—the Patriots were beginning to get a feel for the players they wanted in the draft. None was a workout star.

They liked a center from Boston College, Dan Koppen, who had short arms and whose forty times averaged out to 5.26. They needed help on the defensive line; that wasn't news. But who would have guessed that they were falling for the shortest lineman there? A kid from Temple named Dan Klecko who wasn't quite 5 feet 11½ inches? "Best hands of any lineman in the draft," Licht said. They needed a new Star. They were eyeing Asante Samuel, who was one of the lightest corners at 185 pounds. On his strength reps, Samuel bench-pressed 225 pounds nine times, which tied for the fewest reps in his group of defensive backs. Not good.

It wasn't always about numbers and stats. The Patriots said it and they lived it. It wasn't always about business either. They were starting to feel so good about where they were headed that they found time to fight—playfully. It wasn't that they were excited over certain players. What was more important was that Belichick and Pioli could finally go to work knowing what kind of players they needed and wanted. On Saturday night in Indianapolis, light rain had turned into a heavy rain and snow mixture. Perfect for snowballs. So Pioli and area scout Matt Russell started pelting each other as they ran down Washington Street. Two kids in winter, having fun in the snow.

A few of them had arrived early, even though all they could do now was wait. There were no more grades, alerts, and types for them to put on players. On this Saturday in April, the first day of the draft, the Patriots' scouts were as eager as the fans to see what selections would be made.

It had already been a productive off-season for the Patriots. A productive weekend could, remarkably, have people talking about them as contenders again. Belichick and Pioli had been so good six weeks earlier that they both got handshakes from the boss.

"Nice job today, guys," Robert Kraft had said one evening in March as they all stood near the entrance of football operations. The owner smiled. "Thanks a lot. After spending all this money, my wife can't go shopping now." They smiled back. That day had been incredible. Colvin had been walking around the building, a new Patriot. Cornerback Tyrone Poole would be coming soon. And Rodney Harrison, released by San Diego, was going to join the secondary. It was okay to mention defense to Belichick again. He was starting to feel better. Colvin was going to make them younger, faster, and more versatile on defense. Harrison would bring some toughness and talent to the secondary. Poole could either start or help in the sub packages.

Now, on draft day, Belichick and Pioli had currency.

They had picks. Lots of picks. They had traded Tebucky Jones to New Orleans for three draft choices, a third and seventh this year and a fourth in 2004. The night before the draft they took that third from the Saints and made a swap with the Dolphins: the Patriots' number three for the Dolphins' number two in 2004. They were going into this day with thirteen picks, and the point was not to use them all. Those picks were your passport, allowing you to go wherever you wanted. You could stalk the board, going forward or in reverse, getting who you wanted and where you wanted them.

The best thing about all this flexibility and power was that Belichick and Pioli were content to share it, not fight over it. They knew each other so well that they could effectively communicate with expressions. Pioli knew the difference between Belichick's venting and the coach's serious declarations that a player had to go. There was one assistant coach—Eric Mangini—who could passionately argue with Belichick and then laugh with him later. Pioli was the one other person in football operations who could do the same thing.

It was time for them to get their draft room ready. Their front and back boards—the back board was for prospects who fell below the required 5.50 grade to be a "Make It" player—were set. They had Jimmy Dee stationed in New York, prepared to read the names of drafted players to them. The televisions were tuned to ESPN. The telephones were working. Ernie Adams was at the front of the room, writing out scenarios from the Patriots' "value chart."

Kraft was in the room, paging through some of the information in the massive scouting books. Jonathan Kraft was there too, glancing at the television and reading the business section of the *New York Times*. Belichick was at the center of the room, and Pioli was next to him. Berj Najarian sat several feet away from them. Jason Licht was nearby, prepared to answer any questions about players or draft trends.

As the first round began, there were two mild surprises. The Saints moved up to number 6 to take Johnathan Sullivan, a defensive tackle the Patriots liked. Then, at number 7, the Vikings didn't submit their card before the clock, so Jacksonville and Carolina went ahead of them. When the Vikings did pick, at number 9, they took Kevin Williams, another defensive tackle. Three spots later, St. Louis took defensive tackle Jimmy Kennedy.

The Patriots were two picks away and one defensive tackle they wanted, Ty Warren, was there. They couldn't wait. Some team might be calling the Bears, at number 13, trying to get a defensive tackle as well. Belichick called Angelo. "Hey," he said. "How about a sixth?"

They could talk like minimalists and understand each other. They had known each other since the 1980s, when they were both with the Giants. Angelo agreed, so the teams switched places, with the sixth-round pick as the sweetener. Warren was the choice.

Since the Patriots had another first-rounder, number 19, the phones hadn't stopped ringing. And they had options. Miami was calling again. This time the Dolphins wanted to get into the first round, and they were willing to relinquish next year's first for the right to do it.

"They're clearly going for it all this year," Belichick said to Pioli.

There was a call from Ozzie Newsome in Baltimore. The Ravens wanted number 19—the Patriots guessed they were looking for a quarterback—and apparently weren't willing to pay the necessary price.

"Come on, Ozzie," Belichick said. "Give me a fucking break. Next year's number 1 has to be a part of the deal, minimum. We've already got some action on this pick."

He hung up.

They did have action, but did they really want to make another deal with the Dolphins? They had just taken the Dolphins' 2004 second-round pick, and now Miami was offering its first. A deal with Baltimore would be better by any chart—value or common sense. Newsome called back. If their guy, Kyle Boller, were still there at 19, they'd trade with the Patriots. Arizona had back-to-back picks before them, so the Patriots were tense when the Cardinals were on the clock. They took Bryant Johnson and Calvin Pace. "Thank God for the Cardinals," Adams said. "When you need them to fuck it up, they fuck it up."

It was a deal.

The Patriots dropped twenty-two slots to number 41 and picked up a first for 2004.

Belichick had met with former Dallas coach Jimmy Johnson in the spring, and Jimmy had said a few things that impressed him. Jimmy told him to write down the players he wanted on his team—"Be realistic," Jimmy had warned—and then put together a draft plan from that list. Wasn't the idea to get as many desirable players as possible?

That's what the Patriots were thinking when they moved down. They already had Warren. They could drop down, save money, and pick up two other players on their top-20 list: Eugene Wilson, an Illinois cornerback, and Bethel Johnson, a Texas A&M receiver.

But a run on corners at the end of the first round made them nervous. Pioli started making some calls. First it was the Bengals. "Are you looking to move with this pick?" They weren't. Then it was the Lions. No thanks, again. They finally got a deal with the Texans, one spot behind Angelo and the Bears again. They moved up five spots by packaging their second-rounder with a third they had acquired from Washington. Belichick knew his buddy Angelo needed help at corner. And the Bears did play in Champaign in 2002. He hoped Angelo wouldn't take the local kid, Wilson, at number 35.

"Charles Tillman, cornerback, Louisiana–Lafayette," Dee said from New York. The Bears took him, so now the Patriots could have Wilson.

It was another close one. They made one more deal to secure Johnson—they traded a fourth-rounder to Carolina for the right to move up five spots—and the first day of the draft was done. It was a faultless start, although it wasn't seen that way locally. Fans had wanted to see the Patriots, not the Jets, move up for Kentucky defensive tackle Dewayne Robertson. New England never considered it. They liked what they got on day one. The only day two problem—and a brief problem at that—was an argument between Pioli and Belichick.

Armed with picks, Belichick believed the Patriots could take some chances. Pioli agreed, but not with the particular player Belichick had in mind. Pioli didn't want the player on the board. He thought his character problems were too severe and that drafting him would send the wrong message to the players. Here they had been, for three years, preaching that players conform to a professional standard. How could they turn around and risk that message for an unstable kid? Anyway, Pioli reminded him, think of Cleveland. A few bad attitudes there were enough to sink a couple of teams.

Pioli had convinced him. Instead of risks, they were solid for the rest of the day. They got Klecko, Samuel, and Koppen, their players from the combine. They picked a quarterback, Kliff Kingsbury, in the sixth round and a linebacker, Tully Banta-Cain, in the seventh.

As the day ended Belichick and some of the scouts sat in the draft room. There were no debates or arguments, for the first time in months. It was mellow, with an undercurrent of satisfaction in the room. It was Belichick, Pioli, and a few scouts, sitting around, having a few beers, especially pleased about the state of the new defense. While to some degree of confidence they could predict how the new additions would work out in their organization, what they could not have predicted was the fallout of one player whom many considered the heart of the very defense they'd wanted to improve.

"THEY HATE THEIR COACH"

CHAPTER 11

They got along the first time they met, early in 1996. The twenty-two-year-old kid with the unforgettable name—Lawyer—had impressed Bill Belichick. They had sat down that day and begun watching football films. Three or four hours later they were still going.

Belichick knew then that he liked Lawyer Milloy. It was the way Milloy never lost his focus when they were talking about football. It was the sense that he could watch these films for an additional three or four hours and still want to play afterward.

"I didn't think he had any weak points," Belichick says. "He was one of the most impressive guys I ever talked to. The guy hadn't watched film since his last college game back in November. And shit, he knew everything. 'Here's what this call is, this is why I'm doing this. See that formation? Here are the adjustments. Now he's going in motion, we're checking this, I got him, he's got him. . . . ' It was like he watched the film yesterday."

They put on another film, and it was more of the same. Belichick was an assistant coach with the Patriots then. He knew Milloy, a safety from the University of Washington, could help them. "After what I saw, I thought, *This guy is smart. He's not going to have a problem handling anything.* And he liked football. He was into it. It wasn't work for him. Let's face it: he does have a little bit of an attitude. But in the end you can certainly work with the guy."

The Patriots drafted him in the second round that year. As his position coach, Belichick used to lobby Bill Parcells to start him over Terry Ray. He was ready. They worked together for just one season. After that, Belichick and Parcells were off to New York, and Milloy was left standing in Foxboro, wondering what happened to the Patriots' kingdom that was predicted to come. It didn't. The team went from very good to good, then from good to mediocre. It was bad enough to have a coaching vacancy in 2000, a vacancy that Belichick filled. When the Patriots won Super Bowl XXXVI, two people rushed to Belichick: his daughter, Amanda, and Milloy. "I thought that was appropriate," the coach says.

Even during the good times—when the Patriots were champs—Belichick could always see Milloy's flaws, as a player and as a leader. He really was a leader. And he really wasn't. He brought some of his teammates together. He alienated them. He brought them together again. You just had to understand him. He was full of energy and emotion, a man who spoke it nearly as quickly as he saw it. He wasn't about internalizing his thoughts. He was a glance away from going off, always ready to deliver a lick—verbal or physical.

"A negative leader sometimes" reads the Patriots' 2001 team evaluation report. This was *after* Milloy had helped the team win the Super Bowl. There was also this: "Good production, durable, tough. . . . Over-aggressive, doesn't wrap up, inconsistent leadership, selfish."

There was enough for everyone, depending on your personality and what you were willing to accept. If you didn't mind someone playing his music at his volume near your locker, you liked him. If you did, you had a problem. If you didn't mind a joke at your expense every now and then, you laughed with him. If you couldn't handle it, you shied away. If you were an employee who wished one of the rank and file had the guts to take on management, you adored him. He would say anything to anybody. If you were a designer of fashionable clothing and wanted someone to look good in your clothes, you recruited him. His style was balanced between classic and hip. He had a big heart and a great smile. He was comfortable among the fans and clubs of Boston. He was handsome. A lot of young women turned their heads his way and never turned away.

It gave him and his friend Ty Law immense pride that they weren't sidelined with "soft" injuries. They'd make fun of teammates who would be at practice riding stationary bikes as the two of them put in the real work. Milloy didn't miss any games or many assignments.

He played baseball in high school and college, and he had that quality that a lot of great pitchers have: even when they don't have their best stuff, they make you believe in what's there. And that's what feeds the greatness. Milloy was like that. He made you believe. He was confident and energetic, waving his arms to the crowd. He always had a little more energy than you did, even without his stuff.

In 2002 he was without it.

He was twenty-nine, he made the Pro Bowl—without playing like a Pro Bowler—and in the unfair world of NFL economics he was essentially in his contract year with the Patriots. It is an NFL truism known by all: you don't want to have an average year when you're just south or north of thirty years old. Milloy had an average year. He also happened to be playing for a coach whom he knew as well as the coach knew him. He knew he and Belichick had a lot in common when it came to football, but they couldn't have been more opposite when it came to emotions. The coach observed first and spoke later, if at all. He could go off just like Milloy, but he could also be measured. He was always an economist.

As much as Belichick liked Milloy personally—he was one of the people who sometimes enjoyed the attitude—he didn't like the way the numbers sat on the salary cap. He wasn't thrilled with the '02 production either, but he could have accepted it if it had been next to a cap number different than $4.5 million. Belichick had thought about it the entire off-season. Once, during a draft meeting, scout Tom Dimitroff made a comment about the big plays that he'd seen Milloy make in '02. "I'd like you to come up with some examples," the coach said. "I can't think of any."

Belichick thought about it in March when the Patriots signed former Chargers safety Rodney Harrison, and he continued to think about it in April when safety Tebucky Jones was dealt to the Saints. He wanted the team to negotiate with Milloy's agent, Carl Poston. If they could work out a deal that would give Milloy around $3 million per season, that would be okay.

It was not going to be all right with Milloy. It was a pay cut, and he wasn't interested. On August 19, when the Patriots traded a fourth-round pick to the Bears for nose tackle Ted Washington, it was still an issue. There was almost no chance of the disagreement ending well. New England was halfway through its preseason and three days away from exhibition game number three. Most of Milloy's teammates knew about his contract struggles—he wasn't known for his restraint. They all figured that this season would be his last in New England. They were right: two weeks later, on Tuesday, September 2, per his and his agent Poston's request, he was released. The Patriots had been preparing to do it if a deal couldn't be struck, so they weren't blindsided. Still, now they'd have to explain the loss to the team.

So there was Belichick on one of the most awkward days of the year. He always told the team about roster updates in team meetings. But this wasn't going to be like the day in '02 when he announced that Dean Wells had retired, one day after signing. Lots of players didn't even know who Dean Wells was. This was Lawyer. This was their spokesman for difficult things, the man who would say, "Why are we doing this bullshit?" when other players would think it.

Belichick arrived at the meeting later than usual. He was uncomfortable. He got around to saying that Milloy had been cut and that it was a tough decision. He mentioned that Milloy had given a lot to the organization and that his physical and emotional contributions had made the Lombardi Trophy on the second floor a reality. He gave them the news of the day, waited a few beats, and then started talking about the game they had to play.

The players were stunned.

"Guys were outraged," former Patriots guard Damien Woody says. "The coaches knew it was a volatile situation. Our practices were always loud, with the coaches saying a lot of things. But it wasn't like that the week Lawyer was released. It was quiet. It was that way for an entire week."

What a lot of people would miss later in analyzing the release was that for the players it wasn't all about the departure of Milloy. It wasn't about any trite perception that they were somehow losing heart and soul. They had too much breadth for one player to represent heart and soul. They'd get over the loss. The thing that was so disturbing about the move was that it swung so close to all of them: if Milloy could be cut, following the trade of Drew Bledsoe the year before, who among them couldn't be released?

There was nothing novel about the thought, of course. Players often talk about the business aspects of the league, but they *are* players. They are always taken aback by the shivers of corporate America, shivers that people in other businesses receive from CEOs and COOs. *The company is not doing what we expected, and we're laying off three hundred employees. Effective immediately.* Just like that.

It was tough to be conscious of that coldness and play professional football. That's why every player says it's a business without thinking about it, especially as they give up their bodies while going across the middle. You can devote yourself only to one or the other: pure businessmen will never go over the middle, and pure players will never reduce things to business.

This was not over. They were hurting. They would get

together and prove how tough and professional they were, even if outsiders wouldn't see the results until much later. After the release, there was a defensive meeting—without Belichick present—and players and coaches talked about their feelings.

A few of the veterans stood up and said this was a good lesson for the rookies. Their message to the young players was consistent: "Save your money and take care of yourselves. As you just saw, this can be taken away very quickly." When they were able to sort out the next issue— and when they were able to expertly deconstruct it—they knew they could still be champions.

They began by asking the most relevant question of all: how could they dedicate themselves to an ethic of selflessness and sacrifice when something like this had just happened? They were able to answer that question to their own satisfaction before the meeting was over. They were going to be selfless, not for any altruistic reason but for football.

Selflessness, they concluded, was the most logical and practical way to win games. In a sense, they were being *selfless* for *selfish* reasons, and eventually that insight would make everyone happy.

That was a lot of searching to overcome during an average game week, an extraordinary amount to overcome when a player such as Milloy had been cut, and a nearly impossible amount to overcome when your first game was against the player who had just left.

The Patriots were traveling to Buffalo, where the Bills had a new safety named Milloy. He didn't have much time to practice—only a couple of days—but he still started on Sunday. He was introduced last, wearing his familiar number 36 jersey. He was back to being his energetic self, and he was sparked by the Super Bowl expectations of fans in western New York.

To those who didn't know, it still appeared that the Patriots were torn apart by the Milloy release. They weren't. They were hurt, though, and healing, and now they went straight from the recovery room to violent contact. They didn't have the focus they needed, all the way around, and that sent a couple of false messages throughout the NFL: that the Patriots were a troubled and divided team, and that Buffalo was the best team in the division and on the verge of playing for a championship.

They both looked their parts.

The Bills won decisively, 31–0. The screen passes that had been part of the Patriots' offensive package looked like something out of the 1950s against new Buffalo linebacker Takeo Spikes. He was too fast for the screens and too wise to them as well. Bledsoe had no problem with the "Cover 5" defense that used to include Milloy at the back of it. Tom Brady threw four interceptions. And the leading man, the star of the story, was superb. He made more big plays in game one than he had all of the previous season. He had five tackles, a sack, and an artfully defended pass that he was able to tap to new teammate Nate Clements for an interception.

The severity of the loss accelerated the recovery for the Patriots. There would be a linebackers meeting where Larry Izzo stood up and shouted, "Let's get our shit together." Tedy Bruschi, already a passionate player, would elevate his leadership. Brady, Harrison, Troy Brown, Ted Washington . . . they all took over. Not many people realized that Buffalo may have peaked that day while New England, at least, achieved some clarity from the loss.

"I wouldn't wish this situation that I went through on anybody that plays any kind of sport ever in my life," Milloy told reporters after the game. "Because it was really messed up. But because of the Lord, because of the way my mother raised me, and because of who I am as a person, as a man . . . I was able to not only get through it, but I was able to conquer it. I came out on top."

As the Patriots headed into the second week of the season, the reaction to Belichick's decision fell into two categories outside of the locker room. Essentially, there was either a lot of irony or a lack of context.

Irony because the coach was being criticized for his judgment in two areas where he had shown expertise: the secondary and the salary cap. Irony because it was Belichick's work with the Patriots' defensive backs in '96 that made Robert and Jonathan Kraft pay attention to him more. Well, that and his comprehension of the collective bargaining agreement. He knew when to walk away from a player and knew when to run, either for talent or cap reasons. "You need to understand value in today's NFL," Robert Kraft says. "And he does."

Context because Belichick had made bold and controversial decisions before, without being wrong. He chose Vinny Testaverde over Bernie Kosar in Cleveland, a move that one of his friends equated to "beheading the Browns' mascot." He chose the Patriots over the Jets, escaped the shadow of Parcells, and became known as a great coach away from "home." He chose Brady over Bledsoe and watched Brady become a Super Bowl MVP.

Irony again because he was in Philadelphia—that irony will become clear later—and one of his former players was on national television, saying that his current players hated him.

The Patriots played the Eagles in a 4:15 game at Lincoln Financial Field. That meant they were able to leave their hotel rooms later than usual. They were able to watch the various pregame shows on television, including ESPN's *NFL Sunday Countdown*. At the time the show included Chris Berman and Rush Limbaugh and former pros Michael Irvin, Steve Young, and Tom Jackson. In 1978 Belichick was an assistant in Denver when Jackson was a Pro Bowl linebacker there. Belichick didn't have any memorable exchanges with Jackson then, but—more irony—Jackson and Parcells are friends.

After ESPN aired its story about the Milloy release, including clips from former and current Patriots, Jackson eventually looked in the camera and delivered a line for which Belichick would never forgive him:

"Let me be very clear about this. They hate their coach."

Several Patriots players and staff members saw it, reporters covering the team saw it, and Belichick heard about it. He was furious. It wasn't just that he found Jackson's words irresponsible—Jackson admitted that he hadn't interviewed anyone for his analysis—but he also found fault with the story itself. Eventually he would take his displeasure out on almost everyone at the network. *Almost* everyone because Berman, a longtime friend, was the host of the show.

And this is where the irony of Philadelphia and the Eagles comes in. Limbaugh was still two weeks away from re-signing over comments he would make about Eagles quarterback Donovan McNabb. He was two weeks away from suggesting that McNabb was overrated because the largely white media wanted to see a black quarterback do well. Limbaugh's mere appearance on the show was enough to draw criticism. But on September 14, before the Patriots beat the Eagles 31–10, Limbaugh was the only panelist who supported what Belichick had done. That day the political commentator had been controversial for a different kind of "minority" opinion. His view was that Belichick was not going to make a decision based on sentiment, especially if that sentiment was outweighed by other factors—finances included—that could hurt the balance of the team.

It was common sense for Belichick. He applied this sense so often, with such success, that it was often misunderstood for genius. Belichick's "genius"—a term he does not like applied to himself—is no more than an ability to easily sift through distractions and nonsense and identify the central point. He can even do all of that and come to the conclusion that a central point does not exist. He takes large things and makes them small, which is a strength. Sometimes he believes that large issues, called crises on most teams, can be or should be broken down in the same way with no fallout. That logic could have gotten him into trouble if he had had another kind of team in 2003. He didn't. He had the team with the hidden characteristic, which was simply "professionalism." Supreme professionalism actually.

"As much as some of Belichick's ways can get under

your skin, you've got to give it to him as a coach," Woody says. "We knew that nobody had coaches that were as good as ours. You're talking about a guy who would come into the meetings every week and tell us the three or four things we needed to do to win. 'If you do this, this, and this, you're going to win.' And that's how it would happen."

The meeting in Foxboro following the release of Milloy had been about one thing: professionalism. As a group, the Patriots were not whiners. Belichick was not going to lose the team because they were the team and they were not going to allow themselves to be lost. They wanted to win just as much as he did, and after the first wave of commentaries passed, they knew that the coach and his staff were going to give them a chance every week. They didn't have to love him; they just had to respect that.

Anthony Pleasant had learned about professionalism a decade before when he played for Belichick in Cleveland. Pleasant jumped offside one game, and Belichick took him out and cursed him. The Browns came back to win, and Belichick tried to shake Pleasant's hand afterward. "Man, I ain't shaking your hand," he told the coach. "I'm tired of you messing with me." He went to Belichick's office the next day and apologized. He had been wrong. They shook hands. "It's the way I've handled business with him since then. I go talk to him when I have a problem. At least he will listen. You know, some cats won't even listen."

What Belichick liked about players on his team, he couldn't respect about Jackson. Many of them could admit mistakes, face to face. Jackson never did. He would extend his hand to Belichick on a bizarre February night in Houston. Belichick offered a few words, but not his hand.

"THEY HATE THEIR COACH"

■ ■ ■

After all the talk about Jackson in Philadelphia, the biggest story to come out of the city was an injury to free agent linebacker Rosevelt Colvin. He limped off the field in the second quarter against the Eagles and didn't return. It was obvious that he was hurt, but no one knew it was as bad as a fractured hip. Placed on injured reserve, Colvin was knocked out for the season.

Belichick had spent so much time talking about increasing team speed and acquiring team speed. When the Patriots finally got it in the form of Colvin, they lost it after two games. It was late September, and Colvin and guard Mike Compton were already out for the season. Nose tackle Washington had a broken leg, linebacker Ted Johnson had a broken foot, linebacker Mike Vrabel had a broken arm, cornerback Ty Law had a sprained ankle, and receiver David Patten had a knee injury that would eventually end his season too. Brady had an elbow so sore and swollen that it looked as if he'd had a softball implanted.

No one in Foxboro talked about sympathy or pity because they all knew what the coach knew. They were good and they had depth. "If you look at some of the people we have on our inactive list, they're pretty good players," Belichick said one day outside of the Gillette Stadium cafeteria. He'd stop in there, but he never seemed to be picking up a complete meal. "I'm not saying they're great. But if you look at the inactive list for some teams, you wouldn't even want to put those guys in a game. Our team isn't like that."

His team was smartly built, with one eye on the cap and the other on the field. He was good at figuring out how much better one player was than another and seeing if the price matched the production. Jonathan Kraft, the team's vice chairman, is amazed by his ability to do that.

"Let's say he has a player who has a 100 rating, with really no upside above that. He's a solid 100, he'll be there a few years, he's making $4 million. Bill can see another player who is a 75, making $500,000, and has upside. He knows he can put that kid in a system where the deficiencies between 75 and 100 can also be protected.

"He's never going to get into salary-cap hell chasing that elusive last guy or believing that one person makes your team. He is completely focused on team."

It took a while for his team to catch on locally, though. When they beat the Titans on October 5, it was the same day the Red Sox were trying to tie their best-of-five series with the Oakland A's at two games apiece. And when the Patriots went to Miami and won in overtime—their record was 5–2—everyone in New England was still talking about a silver-haired manager named Grady who refused to take the ball out of his starting pitcher's hand. The region was wounded when the Red Sox lost to the Yankees in the seventh game of the American League Championship Series. In this case, Jackson's words would have been accurate. New England really did hate *this* coach. The Sox led the game in the eighth inning, 5–2, and manager Grady Little famously turned his back to the bullpen and left a scuffling Pedro Martinez on the mound to scuffle some more.

Belichick was a Red Sox fan as well, and he frequently asked for updates on what they were doing. He asked because he liked baseball, but he also liked the challenge of looking at things from all angles to see what he would do. Most of the time he'd take the side of the manager. He loved it in 2001 when Jimy Williams, fired by the Sox, was the first manager hired in the off-season. That was one of the coach's favorite stories. He didn't offer many opinions on Little. He was more interested in seeing if a quick decision—accelerated by public opinion—would be made. A decision came on October 27. Little was out.

Meanwhile, Belichick had a team that was turning him into a mellow coach. These Patriots were much more coachable than his team from '02. They listened. They were resourceful. They didn't make excuses. They had gone to Denver and won, sparked by an intentional safety. That wasn't even the best part of the game. On the winning touchdown, Brady to David Givens, the receiver ran the wrong route. He was supposed to be running a slant and took off on a back-shoulder fade instead. Brady noticed the error immediately and adjusted by throwing for the fade instead of the slant. The players seemed to have a wit and awareness that the coach loved.

This team played each week as if it had something to prove, and Belichick liked that. He respected this team. Whenever someone asked him about the team, he would reply with a rare answer, a "media-ready" answer that actually represented his true feelings. He would tell people that the thing he liked about the Patriots was that they always tried to do what was asked of them. They were students who stayed late after class, determined to figure out some theorem. It sounded kind of plain, but the coach liked their effort.

In case they came down with a bout of arrogance, he was always around to remind them of what they couldn't do. He was good at reminding them to fear the trappings of football success. He could always find a potential distraction and hold it up as yet another Patriots opponent. When it was time to do that in early November, the distraction was close to him. The Patriots were scheduled to play the Cowboys and Bill Parcells on a Sunday night. The players were going to be asked about it. Belichick was going to be asked about it. It was going to be explored from angles obvious and obscure. People were intrigued by Bill versus Bill because the sideline shots were all they got from the story. Everything else was imagined because neither man would get into the specifics of how he was feeling. This was going to be a hard week for Belichick, but it wouldn't be emotional. It would be hard because the actual team was difficult enough to game-plan. Now he would need an effective game plan for comments about Parcells too.

BELICHICK VERSUS PARCELLS

It was one o'clock on a Monday afternoon—November 10, 2003—when Belichick welcomed his team back to Foxboro after an in-season vacation. The Patriots, winners of five consecutive games, had just finished their bye week. On the previous Monday, in Denver, the nation had watched them outwork and outsmart the Broncos on *Monday Night Football*.

The Patriots had trailed by a point, 24–23, with just under three minutes remaining. They were at their own 1-yard line, a few ticks and a few inches away from a loss. After three Tom Brady passes fell incomplete—including one Daniel Graham drop that proved to be helpful—the team was in an obvious fourth-and-10 punting situation. That's when the best special-teams coaches of today and yesterday, Brad Seely and Belichick, decided to give up points to gain an advantage. Long snapper Lonie Paxton hiked the ball and placed it exactly where he wanted it: into the goal posts. New England would hand over the 2 points on the intentional safety, but it would pick up field position on the subsequent free kick and have a chance to retrieve the ball before the two-minute warning.

Special teams, field position, and situational football are all Belichick staples. They were all squeezed into those final three minutes in Denver. So after sitting hopelessly at their 1 with 2:51 remaining, the Patriots were actually able to smile thirty-six seconds later. They suddenly had the ball at their own 42, they had Tom Brady leading them, and they still had time to compose themselves. Predictably, Brady directed a six-play drive that ended with an 18-yard touchdown pass to receiver David Givens. The Patriots won, 30–26. The comeback and the safety left an impression in Denver. "That's a smart play," Broncos defensive end Trevor Pryce told the *Gazette* of Colorado Springs. "I've never seen that done before. That dude [Belichick] thinks."

A few days later Belichick left his Gillette Stadium office for two hours so he could go to Brookline and watch one of his son Brian's football games at Dexter. As he stood on the sideline, waiting for the boys without jersey numbers and face masks to play the game in its most wholesome form, he was noticed by a few parents. They were respectful, understanding that he was there in his role as "Dad" and not "Coach." But that safety was irresistible. "Great job in Denver, Coach," one of the parents said. "What a great finish." Belichick thanked him, talked with Debby, and shouted out, "Nice tackle, Brian," when his son—skinny legs poking out from loose-fitting pants—displayed flawless technique on a takedown.

Belichick had spent his bye week checking in on Brian, Stephen, and Amanda. He had done some self-scouting and game-planning as well. As he stood in front of his players in the Gillette Stadium auditorium on the 10th, the first thing he told them was that he hoped they also had been able to relax. He made that statement shortly after one o'clock. And soon after that, the game resumed. It didn't matter that it was Monday afternoon and the Patriots were scheduled to play the Dallas Cowboys on Sunday night, the 16th. The only people who believe that the games begin on Sunday are the people who watch the games to be entertained. In Foxboro it was time for the business and drama of playing the Cowboys.

It would be the first time Belichick faced Parcells since the longtime colleagues split in January 2000. Both men were storing a lot of emotions, emotions that they were too wise to reveal to the media. They had first worked together in 1981, and that working relationship lasted uninterrupted for a decade. They took a five-year break when Belichick went to Cleveland, but they remained friendly. They picked up again in 1996, and that's when the first signs of wear started to show, just below the shiny surface. Even before football in New York and New England became a Parcells-Belichick docudrama, Belichick had thought of leading a team again—with no link to Parcells.

The next time, he thought, he would do some things differently. He would want to work for an owner with whom he could communicate, and not someone who was easily swayed by the outside opinion of the day. He would want to have some influence over personnel and have someone he trusted leading the personnel/scouting department. He most certainly would hire someone who could help with media relations, his biggest weakness. He just didn't pay enough attention to what was being said and written about him and his team. That was good at times because it eliminated distractions, but it could also undermine what he was trying to do because—whether he liked it or not—it was a part of coaching. And in his first shot at being a head coach, he had left that part of the game unattended. He knew he had the perfect candidate for a position that would encompass several aspects of football operations. The Jets had a public relations assistant named Berj Najarian. Najarian was in his late twenties, grew up on Long Island—he attended Manhasset High, which produced Jim Brown—and graduated from Boston University. Belichick quickly noticed three things about Najarian: he was smart, he was even more organized than the coach (which was hard to do), and he seemed to get along easily with everyone.

Belichick had ideas about a staff. He just needed an opportunity. He got it in 2000, even after Parcells's initial reaction to the Patriots' request to interview Belichick. The official fax from Foxboro to Hempstead, New York, was sent on January 2, 2000, a couple of minutes after Pete Carroll coached New England to a win over the Ravens. Carroll had asked owner Robert Kraft before the game if it was his last day on the job. It was. So the fax was sent before Carroll began his postgame remarks. When Parcells finally saw the transmission from Massachusetts, he scanned it, crumpled it, and continued the conversation he was having. He resigned as Jets head coach the next day, symbolically and contractually handing the Jet keys to Belichick. They were keys that Belichick didn't want because he knew Parcells would always be nearby, jangling the master copies.

As Belichick stood before his players in 2003, he told them that the past didn't matter. He reminded them that there would be a weigh-in the next day and that they were a 7–2 team that needed to be ready for the 7–2 Cowboys. He told them they should know that the Cowboys were leading the league in defense and had 93 more rushing attempts and five more minutes of possession time than their opponents. Well into the meeting he talked about the subject that was going to be topical all week.

Bill versus Bill.

"Don't get distracted by irrelevant aspects of this game," he said. "Belichick versus Parcells? We're both assholes. We started coaching together when some of you were in diapers. The last time we coached together was five years ago. Think about how much has changed in the last five years. What were you doing five years ago and what people were you doing it with? . . . A lot has changed. What happened five or twenty-five years ago doesn't really matter. Nothing could be less relevant to this game or more detrimental to our preparation. Don't get into Belichick versus Parcells. If you want the easy way out, tell them that I won't let you comment."

He made a short detour from that subject, because the no-comment allusion reminded him of injuries. If Belichick is asked about his players' injuries, he tries to guard their confidentiality more than their family doctors might. As much as he likes specificity and certainty in football, he is just the opposite when talking about injuries. He will report the problem area, but in the most general terms allowed. He asked his players not to talk about the injuries to Ted

Washington, Richard Seymour, Ted Johnson, or anyone else. "And it goes without saying, we don't have anything to say—as in nothing—about the play-off race. Nobody knows better than us how quickly things can turn around."

Then he returned to his course.

"If the media want to hype it, great. I'm taking myself out of it. If they want to make this a soap opera, fine. But it will be without me, RAC, Charlie, Pioli, and everybody else with connections—including some of you. Let's figure out what we're going to do about Glover, Ellis, Galloway, Adams, Roy Williams, and Coakley."

He was right about the cross-pollination. It was as if Parcells used to be governor of a giant state that broke off into northern and southern sections. Romeo Crennel, or RAC, had known Parcells since the 1970s, when they worked together at Texas Tech. Charlie Weis had worked with Parcells as a Giant, Jet, and Patriot. During the 1999 season Parcells had taken away Weis's play-calling—he didn't think Weis used the running game enough. There was no shortage of history between New England's head coach, its coordinators, and Parcells. But no one on the team could claim to have Scott Pioli's complex association with Parcells.

Pioli and Belichick were friends when Pioli was in college at Central Connecticut and Belichick was the defensive coordinator of the Giants. Pioli worked for Belichick in Cleveland and spent one year in Baltimore when the "Browns" moved there. With the Jets, Pioli and Belichick had a different dynamic. They were great friends, with offices near each other's, working for the same supervisor. They knew each other's families, worked out together, and participated in office pools. Sometimes one would be treated to an earful when the boss went off on the other. Between Belichick and Parcells, Pioli plainly had more in common with Belichick—until the day he saw a woman with blond hair walk into Parcells's office.

Pioli's question to secretary Linda Leoni—"Who's the blonde?"—was still echoing when Parcells walked out of his office and asked if Pioli had met his daughter, Dallas. He said he hadn't, but he was very glad to now. They talked a lot, found out they knew some of the same people, and had similar interests. They dated. They waited for a while before she would tell her dad and he would tell his boss that each was dating someone Parcells knew. Dallas finally told him, while he was driving, and he reacted as if she had said she was seeing a nice young man from down the street. It was clear that they had his blessing.

The dating went well. It went so well that Pioli decided that he was going to have to get on the boss's calendar for a serious discussion. He couldn't have picked a more hectic day. Parcells was busy, and he wasn't in a very good mood. But Pioli was determined to talk to him. "This had better be important," Parcells said. Pioli was deeply in love with Dallas and wanted to marry her. He told her father that in his office. Parcells was quiet for just a moment, and then he reached out and shook the hand of his future son-in-law.

Eventually that son-in-law would travel to New England with Belichick. And eventually, in the middle of November 2003, there would be sixty minutes of gripping nonfiction. The Cowboys and Patriots would play a physically violent game on the field while a lot of unspoken hostilities played out on each sideline. All the elements were there: love, bitterness, respect, regret. Belichick tried to push it all aside on a November afternoon. Let the critics organize the drama. There was a game to win. "Study up on the Cowboys," he said at the end of the Monday meeting. "I'll have a few questions later."

A *few* questions. Of course, they knew he was understating. On Wednesday he had exactly thirty-two questions about the Cowboys. He randomly went around the room, asking players things they should know about the players they were facing. They did.

Rodney Harrison knew that the Cowboys were more of a play-action than dropback team. The receiving foursome of Givens, Troy Brown, Deion Branch, and Bethel Johnson knew the Cowboys' four main coverages: "Cover 1," "Cover 2," "Cover 4," and blitz zone. When Antowain Smith was asked, "Which linebacker plays to the 3 technique?" he knew the correct answer was Dexter Coakley. Tedy Bruschi knew that on third-and-7-plus the Cowboys went to max protection. And speaking of protections, Mike Vrabel knew the Cowboys were unlikely to favor seven-man protections rather than six.

This is the implicit agreement between the players and coaches every week: we're all going to know what we're doing; we may lose some games, but lack of preparation is an unacceptable reason to fail. That's why Brady sometimes calls Weis at home, asking about plays that could go in the game plan or telling him that he's uncomfortable with some that are in there. It's why Ernie Adams, whose office is a few steps down the hall from Belichick's, often takes a short walk for strategy meetings with the coach. Adams's recall is impressive. He references games from all decades and specific plays from those games that might help the Patriots on

Sunday. It's why all the coaches truly become filmmakers as they study the practice tape. They watch the simulated plays in practice and then predict how the opposing team, based on its identified strengths and weaknesses, will react to the plays. "Does he have it?" is a popular question in the darkened room. That usually means a judgment call: there is some skepticism as to whether a play will work or not. Sometimes "Does he have it?" is a more definitive "He doesn't have it."

This prodding, rewinding, planning, and practicing goes on for hours. It is aided by instinct, research, and computerized trends on what exactly a team does in a given situation. So, for example, Seymour knew what to expect from the Cowboys when they were in the third-and-1 to third-and-6 range: play-action, bootleg, or quarterback run. It was guesswork to some, but not to the coaches. When Belichick, Crennel, and Al Groh all worked together under Parcells, they could look at formations and shout out the correct plays before they happened. If they missed on five calls in a season, they were angry.

There would be no misses on Sunday. The game plan was not complicated. After their analysis of the Cowboys, the coaches came up with the following reminders for the players:

DEFENSE
- Get ahead and take Dallas out of their ball-control offense. Force them to pass to win.
- Disguise coverages.
- Set edge versus run.
- Keep Quincy Carter in pocket.

- Be physical, jam, disrupt, and reroute the receivers—especially number 88 (Terry Glenn).
- Jam number 20 (Richie Anderson).
- No big plays.

OFFENSE

- No turnovers.
- Control the ball.
- Beat man-to-man coverage.
- Pick up the blitz.
- Block number 59 (Dat Nguyen) on runs.
- Third-down conversions.

Belichick told his players not to be distracted by the soap opera, so he literally followed his own advice on Sunday. Television cameras captured him with his back to Parcells during pregame warm-ups. At that time there was no acknowledgment of the man nicknamed "the Tuna." Earlier in the day Parcells had been visiting Scott and Dallas's four-month-old daughter, Mia. Now he was trying to guide the surprising Cowboys to another win, a win that would at least guarantee an even 8–8 season.

The Tuna's former coaches were no dummies. They had put their microscopes on the obvious flaws of his team. They knew they could confuse Carter by mixing three- and four-man fronts. Even if Carter knew what was coming, the Patriots were going to force him to have the most accurate day of his career to win. And if he did those two things, there still was the issue of his running game—the Patriots believed they could stop it too.

Offensively, the Patriots got everything they wanted, and they got it early. Maybe too early, Belichick realized later.

The Cowboys blitzed, as the Patriots expected, which meant man-to-man coverage for the receivers. On a third-and-6 play in the second quarter, Brady threw to Givens, and the young receiver ran for 57 yards. That set up a 2-yard touchdown run by Smith, good for a 9–0 Patriots lead. Brady could have picked apart the Dallas blitzes all day, which was why the Cowboys stopped. And that was a problem.

"Our blitz game plan was effective early and led to 9 points," Belichick explained afterward. "But when Dallas went to coverage, we did not have enough in the passing game to attack them."

So it became a zone game, and the scoring slowed. There were no problems defensively. Troy Hambrick averaged 2.6 yards per carry, Glenn caught one pass, and Carter had a quarterback rating of 38—20 completions, 37 attempts, 3 interceptions. Just like in the old days, the coaches saw the formations and knew what was coming. One adjustment they did make was checking to zone when the Cowboys receivers came out in tight splits. They made the switch so they wouldn't get picked on crossing patterns. That situation came up four times during the game.

There was no way the Patriots were going to lose. They knew what was coming, they knew they had the talent to stop what was coming, and they stopped it. Simple. Belichick had some things to quibble with, such as the 10 unassisted tackles by Nguyen, 4 dropped balls, and 33 yards rushing by Carter. But he was happy. His team won, 12–0. He walked to midfield after the game to greet Parcells, and his former boss surprised him with an awkward hug. Belichick walked off the field and wrapped up another game week with an unemotional press conference. This game—with its buildup and context and personalities—

wasn't like all the others. Some observant and mischievous person on Belichick's staff apparently realized that. When the coach walked through the locker room and into a back office, he saw a small item resting on his desk. It was a stuffed tuna.

With Parcells and the Cowboys off the schedule, there wasn't going to be any other off-field opponent for the Patriots. Playing the rest of the season would be comparatively easy—at least in terms of concentration. The week after Dallas, on November 23, the Patriots went to Houston and won a game they probably should have lost. Trailing 20–13 with 48 seconds to play, they got a touchdown from Brady to Daniel Graham—on fourth-and-1. In overtime the Texans advanced to the New England 40, apparently inching into field-goal position. But Willie McGinest dropped running back Domanick Davis for a 5-yard loss to take the Texans out of range.

Finally, with forty-one seconds left in overtime, they won the game on Adam Vinatieri's 28-yard field goal. "There are at least 1,000 ways to win a football game," Michael Smith wrote in the *Boston Globe*, "and the New England Patriots obviously intend on sampling every one."

He was right. They were 9–2, winners of seven consecutive games. They had Harrison, who did for them what Bryan Cox had done in 2001. Cox was the linebacker who had come on the team and earned respect instantly. Harrison was the same way. He was a gentleman during the week. Sometimes reporters would crowd around his locker and try to ask questions at the same time. "Ladies first," he would say, noticing a female journalist. He would check around the locker room, making sure that players were getting the proper rest and nutrition. "Are you hydrating?" was one of his popular questions. He was one of the players who instituted a fine system for mistakes in games and practices. If coaches made mistakes on calls, they would get fined too. He brought some nastiness to the field. He wanted to make sure that players would remember that the punishment he delivered was different from the average player's. You couldn't find the gentleman during the game.

The defense had gone from one of the league's worst to its best. The Patriots would position now-healthy Ted Washington toward the side of the line where the other team most wanted to run the ball—and the team wouldn't run the way it wanted to. Washington was also a force in defensive line meetings, making sure that other players knew their assignments and what two or three plays had to be stopped. There were cerebral players at every position. The strong-side linebacker, Mike Vrabel, always surprised the coaches by what he was able to remember and what he had the audacity to say. Vrabel could recite coaching notes—"They're ninety-two percent run out of this formation"—and still be instinctive enough to make plays. He was funny too. Once Belichick was warning the players about what the media were going to say to the team. "They're going to come in here and blow smoke up your ass," the coach was saying. "They're going to give you blow jobs, tell you how great you are, they're going to pile it on thick. . . ." He finished talking and looked around the room. Vrabel's hand was raised. The coach braced himself for some kind of comeback.

"Yeah, Mike," Belichick said.

"What was that you were saying about blow jobs?"

The whole team laughed. And there was a good combination of laughter and business during the season. Josh McDaniels, one of the coaching assistants, came up with a Friday segment called "bonus cuts." He would show twenty-five plays that illustrated the key points the players needed to remember. He realized that attention spans were short on Fridays, so he made the package must-see film by adding the bonus cuts at the end of them. Sometimes it was footage of himself and Eric Mangini in high school and Pepper Johnson and Rob Ryan in college. There was a clip from Johnson's brief announcing career in New York. The anchors went to him on a live shot, and Pepper, seemingly surprised, threw up his hand in front of the camera and said, "Hi, guys." The players walked around saying that for weeks. They even included the quick wave to sell the joke, a joke that never got old. Later in the season one of the bonus cuts showed a drawling Joe Namath saying to ESPN reporter Suzy Kolber, "I want to kiss you." That exchange took place in New Jersey, when the Patriots were playing the Jets. The players loved bonus cuts. The three or four times McDaniels didn't include them at the end of his presentations there would be groans in the auditorium.

It was turning into a great season for the Patriots. Their defense was reliable and accountable. And now they were on their way to Indianapolis, where, when it mattered most, they wouldn't relinquish a single yard.

BELICHICK VERSUS PARCELLS

■ ■ ■

This is how quickly things can change in professional sports. Over the course of eleven weeks, "The Lawyer Milloy Situation" had become "The Buffalo Game" for the New England Patriots. Whenever anyone got cocky in Foxboro, the response was always, "Remember Buffalo." There was no mention of the fact that one had helped create the other.

It was an old topic anyway, and few people referenced it. Too many things had changed. Eugene Wilson, the rookie cornerback, was now playing safety with Harrison. Tyrone Poole, whom his teammates nicknamed "Chompers" (he has large teeth), was playing like a Pro Bowler at the corner opposite of Law. In training camp Poole seemed indifferent about being with the team. A religious man, he said God had cleared his mind and helped him concentrate on football again. And Washington, the defensive tackle who liked to shout out, "Mornin'!" for no apparent reason, was back in the middle of a defense that alternated between three-four and four-three fronts.

The Patriots were in downtown Indianapolis, preparing to face the 9–2 Colts. They probably would have been favorites if the game had been in Foxboro. But the Colts were in their climate-controlled comfort, and they were averaging 27 points per game. They were going to be tough to stop.

It wasn't so tough in the beginning: the Patriots took a 31–10 lead into the third quarter. But then the Colts tied it at 31 in the fourth. New England went ahead on a Deion

Branch touchdown, but Mike Vanderjagt's 29-yard field goal made it 38–34. That's when the RCA Dome carpet was transformed into a stage, the venue for one of the most dramatic finishes of the season. When the Patriots couldn't move the ball and had compounded their problems with an 18-yard Ken Walter punt, the Colts had the ball at the New England 48 with 2:57 to play. (Walter was released the next day, after a season of bad punting. During the Patriots' evaluations in '02 one of the coaches had suggested that Walter see a sports psychologist.)

The Colts were moving now, quarterback Peyton Manning pointing and directing at the line of scrimmage. It took Manning two minutes and seventeen seconds to get the Colts to the 2. There were forty seconds left. And if anything justified Belichick's insistence that the defense had to be better, this was it. This was a stand. The ball was six feet away from the goal line. It was also a measurement of a different kind. This was going to show how far the Patriots had come. It was going to show how study and preparation could aid athletic ability.

The ball got three feet closer to the goal after one Edgerrin James run, with twenty-four seconds to play. The coaches had called for Harrison to blitz from the edge. But he noticed that the play was heading inside and changed on his own, stopping James's progress. The Colts tried to run a quick play on second down and sneak James in. But Washington was positioned to the side where the play was to be run, and he was good at splitting the guard-center gap. He led the up-front pushing, and Harrison, Tedy Bruschi, and Wilson stopped James for no gain. There were eighteen seconds left, and it was third down.

Three feet away.

Manning called time. The Patriots knew it was going to be a pass, most likely a fade route on Poole. "Smell shit," Rob Ryan said from the coaches' box. The Colts were bringing in a rookie receiver, Aaron Moorehead, who hadn't been a factor all day. Of course, they were going to him. Wilson told Poole that he would help him on the jam, so Moorehead was out of position from the start. The Patriots were ready for the fade, and it sailed out of the end zone.

Fourth down with fourteen seconds to play and thirty-six inches to defend. The Colts went with James, and McGinest, for the second week in a row, blew up a key play in the backfield. He was able to get there because Washington was in that gap again. If McGinest—who had bluffed a jam and decided to charge instead—hadn't taken out James, someone else would have gotten him.

The Patriots won, 38–34. They weren't a lot better than the teams they played. Sometimes the difference between them and others could be measured in points. Other times it was inches. The wins had begun to take on styles and themes, like the work from your favorite artist. The Patriots were becoming a brand. There was such a thing as a "Patriots' Guy" and a "Patriots' Win." The games were close enough to be dramatic, but physical enough for teams to understand that they weren't going to win.

Consecutive win number 9 was the division winner in the snow, 12–0 over the Dolphins. Fans, with at least eighteen inches of it at their feet, made snow confetti when Bruschi scored the lone touchdown. He got into the end zone and fell to his knees, surprised that he had turned the game with a pluck of a Jay Fiedler pass. As "Rock & Roll Part 2" played, the snow flew into the air on each "Hey!" Number 10 was a knockoff snow sequel—the snow came late—over the Jaguars. Eleven was worthy of an off-off-Broadway location—or New Jersey—against the struggling Jets. Number 12 was destined for song or poem, one with the closing line an ironic twist of the first line.

That's because number 12 was Buffalo. The Bills were 6–9, incapable of scoring consistently. Bledsoe looked bad, nothing like the quarterback who had commanded so much of New England's attention in the Bledsoe-Brady debates. Milloy was not a factor. The Bills, statistically, were worse than they had been the previous year.

They lost to the Patriots two days after Christmas, 31–0. It was a perfect score. Perfect for Jackson, who would occasionally pop up on Belichick's TV saying, "They love their coach!" Belichick didn't think it was funny. Why no phone call from Jackson? No letter? No admission staring into the camera, just as he had done on September 14? Belichick wasn't done with him, and the Patriots weren't done with the NFL. They were going to the play-offs, with the top seed in the conference throughout. They were going to claim the trophy that they couldn't even defend one year before. The next time they went into that auditorium, it wasn't going to be a breakup meeting. They were going to sneak by Tennessee in the cold and beat Indianapolis again, this time in the snow.

Against Buffalo, they knew they had gained some type of redemption. "The way this season went for us was definitely a shock," Milloy told Ron Borges of the *Boston Globe*. "We opened the year beating them 31–0, and now we lose to them by the same score. That puts the exclamation point on the difference between us. I'm ready to go home for a while and just get away from football."

Milloy had not finished on top. Financially, yes. But he was going home to get away from football, and his old teammates were headed to Houston to play more of it. For the second time in three years the New England Patriots were going to the Super Bowl.

PATRIOT REIGN
REVISITED

Between the live music and the conversations of six thousand people, it was difficult to hear anyone talking at the dinner table. You could look at the person sitting across from you and attempt to read his lips, but if you wanted to talk without straining, it was best to turn to your immediate left or right. Since that was the story on a Monday night in Houston, Bill Belichick could have made the case that he had the best seat in the house.

It was January 26, 2004, and Jim Nantz was hosting the first big event of Super Bowl Week at Houston's Reliant Arena. This was a gala celebrating the city's most impressive sports stars, a function so heavy with celebrity that the *Houston Chronicle* correctly noted that Carl Lewis and Hakeem Olajuwon couldn't make it and the star power of the roster still was not diminished. The roll call sprawled like the six hundred square miles of the city itself, from Bum Phillips and Earl Campbell to Roger Clemens and Nolan Ryan to Rudy Tomjanovich and Moses Malone back to Sheryl Swoopes and Mary Lou Retton. This was "A Houston Salute," but it was an event for all of Texas: large, colorful, and bold. For those keeping tabs on karma, it was the first clue that the New England Patriots and the Carolina Panthers were six days away from italicizing the NFL's championship game. *Super* Bowl XXXVIII, without a doubt.

So much had changed for Belichick and the Patriots in the two years since they had last played for a title. They were the subjects of pity and condescension then, a group of players expected to aspire to silver medals rather than the silver Lombardi Trophy. But they beat the St. Louis Rams, earned the trophy, and eventually lost their ability to reside on the margins. They were not the anonymous Patriots anymore. They were not the underdogs. They were winners of fourteen games in a row, the second-longest streak in league history. They could no longer take the position of critical outsiders, here to surprise the privileged of their sport. They *were* the insiders now, and their privilege could be seen in the seating chart for dinner.

Mark Fredland, Belichick's friend from high school and college, sat to the coach's right. George Herbert Walker Bush, the forty-first president of the United States, sat to the coach's left. (Barbara Bush was sitting at a table with Panthers head coach John Fox.) Patriots owner Robert Kraft sat to the left of Bush, and NFL commissioner Paul Tagliabue sat to the left of Kraft. There was no way to downplay it: this table was special. Berj Najarian found that out as he sat across the table and prepared to snap a casual photo of Belichick and President Bush. As soon as Najarian took the picture, he heard disapproving voices: "Hey, hey. . . ."

Two Secret Service men suddenly approached the table.

"He's okay," Dan Kraft, one of the owner's four sons, assured them. The agents were at ease again. There is no such thing as casual or private when a president joins you for dinner.

Bush and Belichick talked about the Massachusetts school they both attended, Phillips Academy in Andover. They remembered that Bush spoke to Belichick's class— the class of 1971—and that one of the coach's classmates was a kid from Texas named John Ellis. Yep. John Ellis Bush, also known as "Jeb." Belichick was impressed with the fullness of the eighty-year-old man's career. Like Steve Belichick, Bush had been an officer in the Navy. He had been a businessman, a member of the House of Representatives, and director of the CIA. He was now a sportsman, into skydiving and football. He was a Patriots fan who developed a friendship with Robert Kraft in the early 1990s; Bush was even at the first regular-season game at Gillette Stadium in September 2002.

As he sat at dinner—surrounded by sports, entertainment, and political celebrity—Belichick had no idea that the entire week would unfold like this. There would be more celebrities sitting, standing, and sometimes controversially performing in the vicinity of his team. There would be more coincidence, a trend that ended with their quarterback and kicker reprising the dramatic moments from New Orleans in 2002. There would be surprises, a mild fight with the league, a frightening close call that would have nothing to do with football, and late-night curses for Tom Jackson and Warren Sapp.

One day after seeing stars at the gala, Belichick was back in a more normal setting. He was having dinner at Houston's, a few minutes away from the Inter-Continental, the Patriots' hotel. Fredland and Najarian were there again—Najarian didn't have a camera this time—along with a few members of the media. Armen Keteyian of CBS, Steve Cohen of WFAN in New York, and Wendi Nix of WHDH-TV in Boston were all able to see a relaxed Belichick cover a number of topics. He is conversant in several areas, so there was no need to cling to football subjects. But with that said, on January 27, Belichick knew exactly what his team needed to do to beat the Panthers. His players felt the same way.

"I felt like I was ready to play the game on the Sunday we landed in Houston," Tom Brady says. "We had an extra week of preparation, and it helped. I felt like I was more prepared for that game than any other one of the year."

There were some things about the Panthers that concerned Belichick. This was a group that had begun to identify with the Patriots of 2001. They believed they were among the toughest and most overlooked players in the league and had not received their proper due all season. They had won two play-off games on the road, including an NFC Championship game win in which they allowed just 3 points to the Philadelphia Eagles. The perception was that they were a conservative offense that relied on the legs of running back Stephen Davis. But Belichick,

Romeo Crennel, and Charlie Weis knew better. They respected Fox, offensive coordinator Dan Henning, and special-teams coach Scott O'Brien, who had been on Belichick's staff in Cleveland. The Panthers were clever with their offense. They would give the appearance of a pure, empty backfield but remix that look by having a six-man protection scheme. They liked to send receiver Muhsin Muhammad in motion to take advantage of his exceptional blocking. They liked "wide routes" where they would pass to the halfback in the flat and suddenly turn the play into a moving screen. The receiver they'd send deep was Steve Smith, who was effective because he was quick and aggressive enough to escape the jam at the line of scrimmage.

They didn't have to be studied and decoded, as the Rams had been two years before. But they were difficult to prepare for because they took the Patriots' approach: they didn't make it easy for you; they made you plan for everything.

The Panthers had one of the most impressive defensive lines in football with Kris Jenkins, Julius Peppers, Brentson Buckner, and Mike Rucker. The foursome allowed Carolina to have defensive depth and range. The Panthers had four versions of "Cover 2" and three versions of "Cover 1." They blitzed corners, safeties, and linebackers. Sometimes they would sit in a zone and let the pressure come naturally from their line.

Tampa Bay had played the Panthers twice in the regular season and lost both times. Warren Sapp, a Buccaneers defensive tackle, believed he had seen enough of the Panthers to know what the difference in the game would be. During an interview with Michael Wilbon and Tony Kornheiser of

ESPN's *Pardon the Interruption*, Sapp said the Panthers' defensive line would overwhelm the men assigned to protect Brady. He threw in a shot at Patriots guard Russ Hochstein, who would have to start because regular Damien Woody suffered a torn MCL in the divisional play-off win against Tennessee.

"I don't even think it's a fair matchup," Sapp said. "I don't see how they're going to get it done, because I think Russ Hochstein started for them in the AFC Championship game, and I've seen Russ Hochstein block, and he couldn't block either of you two fellas. Damien Woody was the best lineman they had, but Russ Hochstein, trust me, my friend, he couldn't block either of you two."

What Sapp didn't understand was that the Patriots had planned for this situation, specifically and generally. They knew when and where Carolina was going to try to shoot the gaps, and they were ready to counter it. They would ask tight end Daniel Graham to stay in and help with the blocking on some plays. At other times they were comfortable enough to have a running back pick up the blitz if it came from the weak side. They realized that the back might be, in certain situations, five-foot-eight-inch Kevin Faulk. The assignment wouldn't be as tough as expected for other reasons too. One was Brady, who could quickly read defenses and change the protection if necessary. "Having Brady is like having Belichick on the field—only Brady has a better arm," Rob Ryan says. It was also a plus that all of the New England linemen were astute enough to make calls. The job wasn't just left to the center.

The larger point, though, was the development program for linemen that the Patriots had written into their scouting manual. It was an outline for those players who weren't ready to contribute but "may be able to compete within a year with strength and development and intense individual technique refining."

Hochstein was not ready to play when he came out of Nebraska, even though he had arrived in Lincoln as a 240-pounder and left as a 295-pound All-American. He still wasn't ready when Tampa selected him in the fifth round in 2001 and then released him a year later. He wasn't initially ready for the Patriots or their offensive line coach when he was signed in 2002. Dante Scarnecchia was similar to many coaches on the New England staff. He wanted things done right, and he wanted you to stay until you got it right. In Hochstein's first year with New England, Scarnecchia didn't think the guard brought enough vigor to his upper-body training. He called him a "bullshitter in the weight room."

All of that had changed by January 2004. Change, in fact, was another Patriots element that was difficult to analyze. They were forever in motion—in a good way. They forced you to update your scouting reports on them weekly, because what you saw two months ago might be irrelevant today. So Sapp was probably right about the '02 version of Hochstein. The Bucs did, after all, give up on him. But he was valuable to the Patriots, and even the man he replaced could see it.

"Russ is like three-quarters of the guys on the line," Woody explained. "He doesn't have the greatest athletic skills, but he's an overachiever, he works hard, and he's smart. That's about it. I think Warren was jealous. We were in the Super Bowl, and he was at home eating a sandwich."

Figuratively, that was true. Literally, Sapp was on the loose at Tuesday's Media Day, the annual breeding ground for the absurd. Sapp had a microphone, an NFL Network camera crew, a bodyguard, and curious members of the media following him around the Reliant Stadium field. He approached Hochstein and asked, "Aren't you glad I made you the center of attention?" Hochstein stared at Sapp and replied, "No more questions." Sapp would later joke about Hochstein moving as if both of his shoes were tied together.

Maybe it wasn't so overt during the season, but the Patriots were used to the skeptics. There was Sapp. There was Tennessee guard Zach Piller, who said he would be shocked if the Patriots won the title. Following the AFC Championship game, when league co-MVP Peyton Manning threw five interceptions, there were complaints that the Patriots might have stretched the rules with all of their contact at the line. The Patriots obviously won a lot, but the feeling was that they didn't win by large enough margins to snuff out the hope of their opponents.

"I don't want to say that we didn't get any respect, because we did," Brady says. "I just don't think a lot of teams felt we were that good. They thought we were good, but not like the 49ers or the Steelers or Cowboys."

That was part of their motivation during the week. They had been reminded many times that they and the Panthers had accomplished the same thing. All they had done, on Wednesday of Super Bowl Week, was qualify for the game. Would they really be considered one of history's great teams if they lost the Super Bowl? Who would be talking about the fourteen-game winning streak then? These were the things they talked about when they went to the second level of the Inter-Continental and held their meetings in Champions Ballroom. They talked about it at lunch, on the first floor, in a room called "Legends." They tried to have good practices at Rice University so they would be ready for whatever Carolina showed them. Their actual practices were good in terms of execution and speed. But there were other problems.

"We can't practice here," Belichick said as he watched his team run. The coach didn't like the layout of the field. Just over a yard away from the playing surface, Belichick saw what he described as drainage pipes. He thought the field was too wet, and after seeing Rodney Harrison do a split—unintentionally—during one sequence, he made up his mind. He was going to the league and telling it that the venue had to be changed. He made his case and was told that the alternative venue was the Houston Texans' practice bubble. It was to be used when it was raining. "Well," Belichick said, "let's pretend it's raining." He was told that the league did not want to favor one team and thus create some type of unfair advantage. He said he was not looking for an advantage. He just wanted to keep his players from injuring themselves on a sloped field that he said "looks like a fairway." Belichick wasn't going to let this one go. He pressed, and the venue was changed.

As the Patriots moved toward the weekend there was more to think about than the condition of the practice field. Belichick had been told by NFL security that there had been an issue at the Panthers' hotel. Carolina was staying at the Wyndham Greenspoint in north Houston, about twenty miles and twenty-five minutes away from the Inter-Continental.

A man had been caught in the stairwell of the Wyndham—on the players' floor—and he was in possession of shells. After a search of the stairwell, a gun was found as well. When Belichick received all the information, he relayed it to his players. He told them that the story was likely to break and that they would be asked about it. He told them to be careful and also emphasized that there had been no security problems where they were staying.

The man with the gun was arrested, but surprisingly, the story never surfaced. (The Houston police department denied a request for the police report, claiming that the investigation is active.) Anyone who was thinking of the possibilities could have been frightened by the story, and anyone who was looking for a motive could have been confused by it. In the days before the game, collectively, the Patriots did neither.

They continued as they had in the past, reciting the tendencies of the Panthers. They knew then that they were not going to be switching to any sub defenses on third down, because they were determined to take away Davis as a runner. And the Panthers were not afraid to run with Davis or DeShaun Foster on any down. The receivers had been told, over and over, that they were going to have to beat man-to-man coverage against the Carolina corners, who liked to play physically. The defenders knew all about Jake Delhomme, the quarterback who may have been more effective when the original plays broke down and he was forced to freelance. He was a good freelancer, but the guys on defense had been told to look for the ball because Delhomme was also a fumbler. The Patriots were becoming experts on the Panthers, and Belichick thought the process was happening at the right time. With the extra week, he didn't want the team to be ready too soon and bored in the days before the game. Now they could have the buildup they needed before pursuing the second championship in the franchise's 44-season history.

On Saturday night at 9:45, one hour and fifteen minutes before curfew, Tom Brady sat in the Houston Airport Marriott. He was eating crab legs and talking with backup quarterback Damon Huard. It was the best conversation they'd ever had. They didn't talk much football, even though the game was less than twenty-four hours away. It was going to be Huard's last game under contract with the Patriots, so they talked about the future and the past.

"He was very much at peace with himself, and that led to a philosophical discussion," Brady says. "We may have mentioned the game for two minutes, but the rest of it was just b.s.-ing about life. I remember thinking, *What a great night, no matter what happens tomorrow*."

He said, "no matter what happens," but he had an idea of what was going to take place the next day. On Friday he and Huard did have a football conversation. One of the comments he made to Huard then was that, throughout his career, the final game of the season had always come down to some last-minute or overtime situation. That's what happened when he directed the University of Michigan to an Orange Bowl win over Alabama, 35–34 in overtime. At the end of the 2001 season he had the drive in the Super Bowl against the Rams. In 2002 he tried to save the season at the end, sore arm and all. The Patriots were down 10 to the Dolphins with five minutes to play, and he led them to a

win in overtime. Why would this game on Sunday afternoon be any different?

That's really the way he looked at it too. It was the game
on Sunday, and if anything, he could handle a game in the
literal sense. His "game" used to make him tense. He is
viewed as a sex symbol now, an image that makes him
laugh when he thinks of all the times he couldn't get a date.
He remembers being shy with a young woman at Michigan, a woman he adored—and a woman who ignored him.
He and his friend Aaron Shea used to drive by her house
and hope that she'd be outside. Brady would see her at
clubs, and she would barely talk to him. Sex symbol? He
thinks of incidents like that when he hears about the
women who want to wear his jersey, frame his picture, or
be the ones who would never ignore him at clubs.

"That's the stuff that makes me most uncomfortable. I'm
very confident as a football player; I have no problems. I'm
not natural with cameras and pictures. Put me in a room
with my family, and I'm the one cracking jokes. Put me in a
room with people I don't know, I'll be a little shy for a while
until I can figure out what to say. What it comes down to is
that I just want to be a great football player."

He is intrigued by complex minds. He goes out of his
way to applaud a good piece of literature, a provocative
film—he was amazed that Mel Gibson could even concep-
tualize a movie about the Passion of Jesus Christ—or an
act of courage. He wants to be a great football player, but
he says the greatness of football doesn't compare to other
things he has seen. He mentions his oldest sister, Maureen.
"She's tough," he says. "I admire what she's able to do."
What she's able to do, Brady says, is be a single mother
who takes care of her children. He recognizes the difficulty

in that, and it's more likely to get his praise than something *he* does at the back end of a game.

But he does play football, and he plays it well. His teammates listen to him, believe in him, trust him. He is the one looking over the game plan on Tuesday nights and saying to himself, *How in the hell am I ever going to get this down by Sunday?* He always gets it, though. He'll be away from the office and call Charlie Weis, wanting to talk about plays. There are some he likes and there are some he would like to tweak. Weis knows Brady so well and trusts him so much that he never forces any plays on him. Once Brady is able to practice the plays and let them run through his mind in practice, he feels like his team can beat anybody's.

"Tom is a cocky sonofabitch," Damien Woody says. "He knows he's going to win, and he makes you believe it. You know what? I'd die for the man. I think you know what I mean. He's the kind of guy who makes you want to bust your ass. He's a great quarterback, a great leader. He's so good that he'll go up to the other team and tell them what he's going to do. I can't say enough about him."

Brady knew on that Saturday night that he could handle the Panthers. He knew what he was supposed to do, and he knew what the team had to do. He had been ready to play for a week. He was certainly ready when Crennel began his curfew checks at eleven o'clock.

When he awoke early Sunday morning, Brady immediately went into his routine. He had an iPod programmed for the special day. He had thirty-eight songs for Super Bowl XXXVIII. Jay-Z was on there, along with Aerosmith, Kid Rock, and 50 Cent. He had already grasped, from his first Super Bowl trip to New Orleans, that there wasn't any reason to be nervous. The early bus would be leaving for Reliant at 1:15, a little more than four hours before the start of the game.

Belichick had been as confident as Brady on Saturday night. He kept looking at the things Carolina did well, and he feared the potential of those things. He did fight his overconfidence a bit, though, because he saw some weaknesses on the Panthers. He saw those weaknesses and visualized his team pouncing on them. He never thought that once more tilting the game the way he wanted it would almost force Delhomme to win it, or that he would watch the quarterback nearly pull it off.

All the players were there on Sunday, the first day of February, at noon. They reviewed what they were going to do. They viewed the trophy some of them had worked for in New Orleans. Others had recognized it from television, pictures, the Gillette trophy case, or long reminiscences on the team plane. They wanted to get their own so the team could be united in its philosophy as well as its hardware.

They arrived at the stadium with the retractable roof, and the question at that time was simple: open or closed? It was cloudy and cool—for Houston—so playing in 60-degree weather was going to be a game-time decision. The roof would be closed, but aesthetically it wasn't going to matter. The stadium was beautiful. This was a Texas building, super-sized in every category, from price—$449 million—to length of the video boards—360 feet.

Most players agreed that it was hot on the field, so it was easy to get warmed up. As those warm-ups took place and then came to an end, there was a different kind of heat on the field. Belichick was standing next to defensive tackle Richard Seymour, and they both noticed it.

"Did you see that shit?" Belichick said to Seymour.

"Yeah, I did," he answered.

What they saw was a group of Panthers—"Deon Grant and a couple of other assholes" is the way Belichick put it—trying to stare them down. The tone would be set for both Belichick's pregame speech and the first several minutes of the game. Belichick had wanted to say something anyway after hearing the Panthers compared to the Patriots. He had asked his team all season not to give opponents any material to use against the Patriots. But he wasn't holding back now. He told the team that he was tired of hearing about the great Carolina defensive line, the great receivers, and the tough corners. He said he was tired of hearing that the Panthers were the '01 Patriots.

"It's a bunch of bullshit," he said, his voice rising. "They're not what we are. They can't be what we are. *We* are what we are."

"This is going to sound weird since it was a lot of expletives," Woody says, "but it was touching. We saw a different side of him. We had never seen him that emotional before. He got me ready. I felt like going out there, strapping it up, and playing on one leg."

Woody left the playing to Hochstein and the rest of the Patriots, who decided to come out as a team. The Panthers decided to do the same thing. So there they both were, standing in Texas, minutes away from playing one of the oddest and most exciting of all the Super Bowls. They were about to walk the line between boxing and ballet, pounding each other on one series and floating by one another on the next. "It was as physical a game as I have ever seen," says Armen Keteyian, who watched from the sideline. "It was an all-time Texas steel cage match."

There was just one sweet thing between the Patriots and Panthers, and it was the voice of Houston native Beyonce Knowles. She sang "The Star-Spangled Banner" angelically. But it was an evening when the sounds—well, the *appearance*—of pop musicians could not be innocent, and the nation would debate that on Monday morning more than the game. As for the game, all indications were that it would be a low-scoring one. It just made sense when you put the teams side by side. Neither one had a head coach or an offensive coordinator with a drop-back-and-let-it-fly mentality. The Panthers liked to run, and the Patriots had allowed just one 100-yard rusher all season. The Patriots were going to try running as well, and there was that line that everyone had heard about.

So when the teams nearly went the first twenty-seven minutes without scoring, it seemed to be turning into a game that was on its way to a 14–10 finish. Patriots receiver Troy Brown had his nose broken early and still went back in the game. Adam Vinatieri, with a portfolio of winning kicks, already had missed two field goals in the first half.

The first one he described as a simple miss, from 31 yards away. Shane Burton blocked the next attempt, which was a 36-yarder. Belichick didn't like this. He had said earlier that Scott O'Brien, the Carolina special-teams coach, knew some of the Patriots specialists better than he did. O'Brien had coached long snapper Brian Kinchen and holder Ken Walter. With an injury to regular snapper Lonie

Paxton and a fitful season of punting by Walter—he had already been released and re-signed during the season—part of the Patriots' kicking game was damaged.

Vinatieri wanted to be accepted as a football player, not the temperamental kicker-in-residence, so he didn't complain about a couple of things that were bothering him. He was hurting, with constant pain in his back. And with the injury to Paxton, his timing on his kicks was thrown off. He, Paxton, and Walter had practiced so much together that they never had to think about the technical aspects of their jobs. It was part of their muscle memory: straight snaps by Paxton, clean catches and quick placements by Walter, stress-free kicks by Vinatieri.

Finally, with just over five minutes left in the half, the Patriots got what they wanted and expected. Mike Vrabel, the defense's quick-witted scholar, sacked Delhomme at the Carolina 19. He jarred the ball loose, and Seymour recovered it. Four plays and two minutes later, Brady threw a short touchdown pass to Deion Branch.

Game over, some must have thought. It was that kind of game. Except it really wasn't what it appeared to be. Fans were going to love it for its unpredictability. Coaches were going to look back, reluctantly, and see all the mistakes that made it so dramatic. It was one of those mistakes that led to a tie with seventy-four seconds left in the half.

Patriots corner Tyrone Poole was supposed to jam Steve Smith at the line, and rookie safety Eugene Wilson was supposed to be helping with over-the-top coverage. Neither happened. Poole missed Smith at the line, and Wilson went to cover for Ty Law. Law had told him that he had an idea of what Carolina was trying to do, and he needed Wilson to get his back. Geno, as the rookie was called, didn't go where he was needed. So Poole was left alone on a 39-yard touchdown pass.

As halftime approached, the energy changed again. The Patriots were able to squeeze in a Brady-to-Givens touchdown, and the Panthers were able to get a 50-yard field goal from John Kasay—set up by a 21-yard Davis run—as time expired.

Twenty-four points in three minutes and ten seconds. The Patriots led 14–10 at halftime, and halftime was when pop singers introduced a new phrase to pop culture: wardrobe malfunction. Janet Jackson and Justin Timberlake had been performing "Rock Your Body," a song that includes the lyrics: "Bet I'll have you naked by the end of this song." It turned out to be a solid bet, because toward the end of the performance Timberlake pulled Jackson's bustier and more than a hundred million viewers saw her right breast exposed. It was covered by a nipple shield, but it wasn't covered enough to prevent a stream of complaints, apologies—and Internet searches for close-ups of Jackson's breast. Jackson said it was a wardrobe malfunction, and she and Timberlake issued apologies.

For those watching at home, it would have been understandable for the malfunction to be the buzz of the third quarter. Once again, the teams were trading field position but not points. It was a scoreless third.

When Antowain Smith scored seven seconds into the fourth to make it 21–10, it was time to bury the Panthers again. The Patriots weren't going to blow an 11-point lead, were they? They would in this game of sudden eruptions. "One of the great Super Bowls of all time," wrote *Boston Herald* columnist Gerry Callahan, "broke out like a fistfight in the middle of morning Mass."

Foster had scored on a 33-yard run—Carolina went for a 2-point conversion and failed—and Brady had thrown an interception at the Carolina 2. With the Patriots still leading 21–16, Wilson guessed wrong again and literally got hurt along the way. The Patriots defensive backs had been told that if Delhomme was looking in one direction, he would probably throw in that same direction. So on third-and-10 from his 15, Delhomme looked right. Wilson followed his eyes and cheated right with him. The quarterback couldn't find anything. The play was officially broken. He began to freestyle, and Muhammad was smart enough to freestyle with him. The play wasn't meant to be a GO route, but it became one, and Wilson was in no position to stop it. Eighty-five yards and a missed tackle later, the Panthers had the lead. Wilson was out of the game with a torn groin. Again, the Panthers went for 2 and failed. But they led 22–21.

"Motherfucker!" Brady shouted from the sideline. "I can't believe we're losing."

Brady had gained so much respect from his teammates by pointing out his own errors. His management style was not to berate following a mistake. He liked to mention that the next play was a good opportunity to correct any previous errors. That's what he did after his interception. He began at his 32, mixed five completions with three runs, and led the Patriots to the Carolina 1. That's when the comedian, Vrabel, checked in as an eligible receiver.

"Holla at your boy," Vrabel said in the huddle.

It was not a problem. All Vrabel had to do was hold on to the 1-yard pass, and he did. When Faulk took a direct snap and ran up the middle for the 2-point conversion, it was 29–22 New England. But there was too much time and not enough resistance in this fourth quarter. Wilson was down, and the other safety, Harrison, would soon follow. Harrison broke his arm with just over two minutes left and remained in the game to make the next tackle. He was every bit the player New England expected when they signed him in March 2003, but he could not defy his body. His right arm was drooping, and it was impossible for him to stay in the game like that.

Delhomme went to work on the defense, a defense that was mottled by injuries and mistakes. With seventy-three seconds left, a misunderstanding—Asante Samuel was playing zone when he should have been in man—led to a 12-yard Ricky Proehl touchdown. It was Proehl who had scored the final St. Louis touchdown in Super Bowl XXXVI to tie the score at 17. He was part of a different tie this time: 29 apiece.

"Well, you asked for it," Huard said to Brady before walking away. He did ask for it. He had talked about it on the way to practice on Friday. But this was much deeper than Friday. This went back to Ann Arbor, when he believed he was entitled to run the two-minute drill perfectly. If he were going to be a quarterback, he would have to be skilled at this drill. It's the same way some musicians feel about playing the standards. There are certain crowd-pleasers that have to be in your rotation if you're going to make it in the business.

He was calm. He didn't know most of the 71,525 people here, but this didn't count as an anonymous crowd that could make him nervous. This was still football, and no matter how much importance was placed on this game, it was his game. And, oh, it really belonged to him after Kasay made the biggest mistake of his career. He kicked off, and the ball landed out of bounds. So now twenty-six-year-old Tom Brady, who was already the MVP of one Super Bowl, was a couple of completions away from snatching another one. He was going to begin at his own 40 and have sixty-eight seconds to perform.

Time for the drill. Weis's voice was in his helmet, and that's all he could hear. He was operating from the shotgun. He missed on his first pass, "O Out Cluster 146 Z Option X Deep Return," and then connected with Brown for 13 yards to the Panthers' 47. He wasn't flustered when a 20-yard completion was taken away from him and Brown was called for offensive interference. "Tommy," he heard Weis shout into the helmet. "'Gun Trips Left 259 Max Squirrel X IN.'" He was going back to Brown, for 13, and back on the Carolina side of the field.

Rob Ryan was right. Brady was similar to Belichick in the way he was able to think quickly without *reacting* too quickly. He'd take what he was given. Four yards to Graham, and he was at the 40 with fourteen seconds left. He took a timeout there and still had one left. On third-and-3 from the 40, he picked up 17 yards in five seconds. The play was "Gun Trips Right 80 Rock OPEQ." Deion Branch caught the pass, and New England used its final timeout.

There were nine seconds left. Nine seconds left, and suddenly it was as if a photographer were trying to re-create a family photo from a couple of years ago. *No, you were standing over there the last time. Remember?* Gil Santos was once again describing the scene to listeners in New England. Robert Kraft and his family were in their box. Some coaches were above the field, and others were standing on the sideline. Just like the last time. Nine seconds left, and this time the only difference was that they were more complete than they were in New Orleans. They knew how it felt to win and then be pushed back to mediocrity. They were wise men now, capable of telling you about the joys and burdens of winning. Who among them would take this for granted? Not after what they had seen since February 2002: a new stadium, new teammates, dismissed veterans, frustrating games, loved ones gone too soon.

Vinatieri took the field stuffing his size 11s into a size 9 shoe. There would be no slippage that way. It was going to be foot on ball for ultimate accuracy. This attempt was going to be 7 yards shorter than his winning kick at the Superdome. There would be no talking this time as he walked on the field—the line of scrimmage just on the nose of the 24—and began to create another piece for his collection. The snap was straight, the hold was clean, the kick relieved stress. It was high and good, once again, just like the last time.

In the postgame happiness, there were still harsh words that needed to be said. Belichick was asked twice by ESPN reporters to do one-on-one interviews. Twice he declined. There were celebrations and tears everywhere. The Patriots had won 15 games in a row, allowing them to consider a couple of questions with no wrong answers: How great were they, historically? And which of their two trophies, fingerprinted by family and friends, carried the better story?

Belichick would talk about these things with others, but not, initially, with ESPN. When his friend Chris Berman personally asked him to appear on the air, however, Belichick couldn't turn him down. They walked on the Reliant Stadium field, passing a few workers and television reporters doing stand-ups. On the set Belichick saw Tom Jackson. The coach didn't want to be diplomatic. He still didn't like the way the comment from September was handled, and winning the Super Bowl wasn't going to change his mind about that. Jackson extended his hand to Belichick. The coach looked at him and said, "Fuck you." It was left at that. Belichick went on the air with Berman—Jackson did not join them—and eventually returned to his suite at the Inter-Continental.

The hotel's Discovery Ballroom was where the team party was being held. A proud Tedy Bruschi walked the perimeter of the room, clutching the trophy and allowing fans to touch it. He was smiling and looking for people who wanted to be close to the trophy but didn't have the chance. Some of the musicians from Brady's iPod playlist—Kid Rock, Aerosmith, Snoop Dogg—performed at the party.

Well after midnight Hochstein was spotted walking around the hotel. He was jubilant and drunk, and he waved when a few people called his name. "Hey," he slurred. "Where is Warren Sapp now? Fat motherfucker." He laughed. He had been waiting to get that out for a while. He was a champion, on a team of unlikely champions.

But then, didn't it all make sense that the Patriots would finish like this? This was a team led by a man who sees a link between high production and preparation. He is a man who was raised near an academy where men and women always talk of teamwork and excellence. He took the parts of the structure he liked and fashioned a life in which he would always seek a person's ideas first.

He can never be accused of being distracted by superficial things. Some of his friends are famous and some are not. Some are conservative and some are liberal. He has talked with presidents and prisoners alike. He has made decisions that have been interpreted many ways, but he is not concerned with shaping the interpretations. He is a lover of many things, but football occupies him. He wants to work with people who care about this sport as much as he does. So he has reached out to Robert Kraft, Scott Pioli, Ernie Adams, Eric Mangini, Tom Brady, Richard Seymour, Tedy Bruschi, and Willie McGinest. Anyone can join the club. You just need to have the mind and heart for working. And winning.

EPILOGUE

On the noon plane from Houston's Ellington Field to Boston's Logan Airport—the plane carrying the Super Bowl champions—there still was work to be done. Belichick began some of it by talking with outside linebackers coach Rob Ryan. He told Ryan that the Oakland Raiders had called, and they were asking about him.

The Raiders were looking for a defensive coordinator, and he was one of the candidates. Belichick reminded Ryan that he always had a home in New England, a statement that made the assistant coach smile. But the idea of leading a defense was exciting to him. He was the same kid who once described himself and his twin brother Rex as "the thugs of Canada" when they were living with their mother there. When the twins moved back to the States to live with their famous father, Buddy, they still had some rough edges. Rob remembers taking the ACT for Rex while his brother went fishing. He was the same young man who loaded Burger King trucks for extra money, who once said that the only nonfootball job that appealed to him was border patrol, who had spent so much time working that he and his wife, Kristin, "never had a honeymoon."

If the job were offered, he would have to take it. It was, and he did. (He and Kristin also got their honeymoon: Willie McGinest, who was selected to the Pro Bowl, paid their way to Honolulu.) Ryan left the coaching staff, and so did John Hufnagel, the quarterbacks coach who had been in Foxboro for a season. Hufnagel became the offensive coordinator of the New York Giants. The Patriots were and are loaded with coaches who could lead their own Cabinets, but not everyone got the call he sought. Coordinators Charlie Weis and Romeo Crennel interviewed for head-coaching jobs before the play-offs started, and both, remarkably, were passed over. Belichick knew both men were capable of running teams and implementing original ideas. He also knew he was going to have to do a lot of managerial balancing in the next several months.

There were going to be qualified people—Weis, Crennel, Mangini—performing jobs that they were close to outgrowing. There were going to be tough decisions to make on free agents. Antowain Smith, the back who ran well in two Super Bowls, did not have the option year in his contract picked up by the team. Damien Woody, the team's most talented offensive lineman, was not re-signed and moved on to Detroit. "I'll never forget what I experienced in New England," Woody says. "I hadn't been on a team like that since high school. We would hang out together, have fun, and hold each other accountable. It's something that can never be taken away from me."

EPILOGUE

Ted Washington, who had been close to re-signing with the Patriots, got a better deal in Oakland and followed Ryan there. Cornerback Ty Law, who intercepted Peyton Manning three times in the AFC Championship game, said he no longer wanted to be a Patriot. Law didn't believe he had contract security—given what had happened to Lawyer Milloy—and wanted the Patriots to do something to put him at ease. Both sides talked about a new contract, but a stalemate became public in the second week of March. Law said Belichick lied to him about negotiating and added that the love was gone in New England. He was tired of many things—such as the Patriots' refusal to pay his off-season workout bonus, even though he didn't work out in Foxboro. His contention was that the previous management team, led by Bobby Grier, gave him the bonus anyway.

Belichick released brief statements on some of the transactions and offered no comments on others. He was amused, for the second April in a row, when his team was mentioned in a move-up-in-the-draft rumor with the Detroit Lions. He was supposedly after University of Miami safety Sean Taylor, a rookie he would have to pay more than Milloy and Rodney Harrison if he traded up to get him. And if he did that, he and Scott Pioli would have to make an exception to the draft advice Belichick had received from Jimmy Johnson on his boat, which was to write down all the players you wanted on your team, whether they were in round one or round seven. Belichick had listened to that advice in 2003. He walked away with one of the best drafts in Patriots history.

He applied the same theory to the draft of 2004. He sat at his Gillette Stadium computer and wrote down the names of twenty-five college players he wanted to see on the Patriots. He put them into two categories: first- and second-day draftees. If he and Pioli needed to move up and get a specific player, they had enough capital—or picks—to control the draft board. They had already traded one of their second-round picks to Cincinnati for running back Corey Dillon to replace Antowain Smith. They had also given up a sixth-rounder for defensive lineman Rodney Bailey, who had played the 2003 season in Pittsburgh and would now add depth to their defensive line. Now they had a plan to strengthen the Patriots with draft choices.

The Patriots held two picks in the first round, numbers 21 and 32. At the top of Belichick's list were four players the Patriots should consider moving up for from 21: cornerbacks DeAngelo Hall and Dunta Robinson, defensive tackle Vince Wilfork, and linebacker Jonathan Vilma. Next, he had written "My Card," with "guys I would like to have on 1st day and 2nd day" in parentheses. His first-day card included two tight ends, Ben Watson and Kris Wilson. Three offensive linemen—Chris Snee, Travelle Wharton, and Sean Bubin—were on the list. In addition to Wilfork, he listed nose tackles Marcus Tubbs and Isaac Sopoaga. His linebackers were D. J. Williams, Dontarrious Thomas, and Jason Babin. If he couldn't get Hall or Robinson on the first day, he thought Ahmad Carroll would be a good choice at corner. Taylor was not one of his safeties, but Guss Scott, Madieu Williams, and Dexter Reid were. He rounded out his first-day list with running back Kevin Jones and defensive end Marquise Hill.

Unlike 2003, when the Patriots were dealing to secure their targets, they were quiet in 2004. It was one of those Aprils in which the board was unfolding favorably. They didn't have to move to get what they wanted. Wilfork fell to them at 21, and Watson was there at 32. Snee, Thomas, and Madieu Williams all went to other teams in the second round, but the Patriots were able to get Hill with the 63rd overall pick. Wharton went to the Panthers at number 94, but Scott was right behind him for New England at 95.

That was it for the first day, and three high-priority players—Reid, Sopoaga, and Bubin—remained on the board for the Patriots to select. Day two was impressive: Reid, Christian Morton, Cedric Cobbs, and P. K. Sam—Belichick had written of Sam, "This will be a cheap receiver for four years if we are right"—were drafted. All had been on the coach's list.

It said it right there, in black and white, that the off-season had begun successfully. Jimmy Johnson would have been proud. There was another trophy added to the collection on the second floor, which really meant that there was another piece of hardware to defend. The 2004 Patriots would have to protect their championship *and* their standing as one of the smartest, fairest franchises in professional sports.

ACKNOWLEDGMENTS

This is my first book, and it wouldn't exist if it weren't for dozens of smart, supportive, and visionary people. I realize I just put a lot of pressure on myself with that phrasing—I'm almost guaranteed to forget someone who deserves to be mentioned. But honestly, there isn't enough space to thank the people who made this book come to life. Mauro DiPreta, my editor, tops the list. He did a brilliant job of listening to the original idea and then expanding and organizing it until it became what you are now holding. My literary agent, Basil Kane, had confidence in the manuscript, even when the 2002 Patriots won nine games and the project appeared to be doomed. I'd like to thank the New England Patriots, a secure organization that granted me access without ever asking for or even hinting at editorial control. The Kraft, Belichick, Pioli, and Najarian families were especially helpful and generous with their time.

ACKNOWLEDGMENTS

Eric Mangini was kind enough to teach me defensive concepts on Friday afternoons. The other assistant coaches, scouts, and players were notably professional as an outsider peeked into their world.

Instead of naming each of my family members, I'll just thank my crew—the Holleys, Sales, Soberanises, and Robinsons—for their support.

There are many others to thank. Among them: Terry Pluto, Armen Keteyian, Don Skwar, Stacey James, Joe Amorosino, Jay Muraco, Joanne Chang and the crew at Flour Bakery + Café, the *Boston Globe*, Michael Smith, Ross Carey, Joelle Yudin, Karilyn Crockett, Nick Carparelli, Bob Quinn, Michael Price, Kari Barclift, Golden Touch Secretarial Services, Jackie MacMullan, Dr. Katharine Henderson and Point Park University, and Amanda Abreu. I'm sure there are some names missing. All I can say is that I most likely love you and will include you in the acknowledgments of book number two.